Library and Archives Canada Cataloguing in Publication

McGhee, Robert, 1941-

The thousand-year path : the Canada Hall at the Canadian Museum of

Civilization / Robert McGhee.

Issued also in French under title: Un chemin de mille ans d'histoire, la salle du

Canada du Musée canadien des civilisations.

ISBN 978-1-100-10786-8

Cat. no.: NM24-22/2008E

1. Canadian Museum of Civilization. Canada Hall. 2. Canada—History--Exhibitions. 3. Museum exhibits—Canada.
I. Canadian Museum of Civilization II. Title. III. Title: Canada Hall at the Canadian Museum of Civilization.

AM101.G37M43 2008 971.0074'714221 C2008-980330-2

Published by the
Canadian Museum of Civilization Corporation (CMCC)

100 Laurier Street
Gatineau, Quebec K1A 0M8

Design: Greenmelon Inc.
Printer: Lowe-Martin Group, Ottawa, Canada

the Thousand-Year Path

THE CANADA HALL AT THE CANADIAN MUSEUM OF CIVILIZATION

Robert McGhee

C. Worsnam   C. Elizabeth

Hol de Withheop   Loinle Inlet

C. Harles

Terres de la Brador

Esquimaus

La grande baye

F R A N C E   Sauuages Berssa multa   Le Golphe St Laurens

Montagnaes   Port neuf   Bassc de Ste Marie   Port aux Ours   Terre neuue

Petite nation des   Gaspay
Algommequins   Baye des molhes

Les trou rusieres   Isle percée
                                    Isle bonne auenture
Algomme[ouine]   Sault   Ban des orpholins
                                                    Isle aux oiseaux
Liou ou il y a forse   Sault   Miscou   Isle Brion   Isle ronce
Cerfs   regatay
Harets   Nouuelle   France   baye du petit nsfumhy   La Magdelene   St Paul Rocher
                                                    St Laurens
Lac St Louis   Etechemins   Isle d' Iran   Noant   Isles St Pierre
                    S. Croix   C. des mines   Cap breton
        San fouge   Pemetegoit   Quenis   Poutrincourt   Sourricous   Conceau   Port le faualette   Banquereaux
Hire coir   Port royal
                            Isle longue   Baye Ste Marie   Cap forest   Port de Ste Helaine
                                    Horssuner   Isle de mortier   Baye de toute Isle
        Cop des Isles   Cap forest   Isle defumbre   Port au moutton
                    Beau port   Isle auchangueu   C. de la heue   Isle de sable
        Habitation de Samatec   Port St Louis   Isles aux loups marins
        maniganasticouet   Baye blanche
                    Cap. blanc
                    Moulle barre
                    Port fortuné
Caranteuan mai   Riuiere de Champlain
                    Baye de nostre Dame
        Isle de l'Ascension

10 20 30 40 50 60 70 80 90 100

Faicte lan 1632 par le sieur de Champlain

C. Harles

C. Henry

Table of Contents

Preface

This book does not pretend to be a summary of Canadian history. Rather, it takes its form from the Canadian Museum of Civilization's Canada Hall, which is constructed as a tour along a single meandering trail through time and space. The path begins ten centuries ago, with the first recorded ventures of Norsemen to the coasts of Labrador and Newfoundland, and follows the expansion of European and Euro-Canadian society westwards across the continent and through time. From the trail, the traveller catches glimpses of early post-medieval cod-fishing and whaling enterprises along the Atlantic Coast, the fur trade on the St. Lawrence River, the farming settlements of Acadia and Quebec, and those of the Loyalists who retreated to Canada after the American Revolution. The traveller joins a nineteenth-century Métis buffalo hunt on the eastern Prairies, witnesses the massive changes brought by the railway and the waves of agricultural immigration that expanded the Canadian nation across the west, and observes the unique social and ethnic battles that brought British Columbia into being. In following such a narrow trail, the traveller overlooks a great deal: the long and complex history of Canada's Aboriginal peoples is mostly beyond the traveller's field of vision, as is the history of Eastern Canada after the eighteenth century and that of Central Canada after the nineteenth century.

However, this narrow view of an immense and complex subject does have its advantages. It allows the traveller to focus attention on unique societies and events, as they were experienced and as they may be reconstructed by historical imagination. And, even from such a limited selection of past occurrences, the historical explorer begins to sense themes that are common to many times and places: the vast amount of sheer physical labour that was required to build a country, the privation and intense isolation suffered by so many of our ancestors, the recurring intolerance that developed between ethnic and religious groups, eventually subsiding only to be replaced by fresh sets of fears and prejudices. The traveller along this path can't help but notice the deep historical roots of many of today's concerns: the decline of the Atlantic fishery, the cultural divide between French and English, and the discrepancy between the resource wealth and the political influence of Western Canada. But beyond the turmoil of political dispute, ethnic fears, and hard and dangerous work, the explorer also senses the satisfaction of people who have created productive farms, built comfortable communities, and provided easier lives for the next generation.

The story of any nation is a strange combination of events that seem to have been unavoidable, developing inevitably from previous circumstances, together with other incidents that appear to have been purely random or erratic. This unpredictable mix of events and processes, of cultures and personalities, allows historians to construct countless different interpretations of national history. The interpretations favoured by this author are embedded in the stories within the following 15 chapters. We hope that these glimpses of the past will allow travellers along this historical trail to build their own sense of where the country has come from, and where we might expect it to go.

Riseland

Naxvoe

MARE GLACIALE

Biarmaland

Huidserk

Norvegia

GROENLANDIA
Herioffnes

Island

Feröe

Frisland
H

Hetland

Helleland

Winlandiæ

Orcades

Markland

SIUR"
di Stepha
nü terrarum
hyperborearū
delineatio
Año 1570

IR
LAND

BR
I
TA
NNI

Skrælin

1. *Norse Ventures*

July A.D. 986

It was late in the season to be setting off into unknown waters, especially with only the vaguest of directions, but the young skipper of a small merchant ship had good reason to set sail. Bjarni Herjolfsson had spent the winter in Norway and, in the spring, had loaded his ship with a variety of goods that would bring a good price among his Icelandic countrymen, and sailed home. The voyage had gone well but, when he arrived at the family's farm in southwestern Iceland, he was shocked to find the farm sold and his parents gone. The previous summer, the murderer Eirik the Red had returned from a three-year exile, which he had spent exploring to the west of Iceland. He had reported the discovery of a huge country of glaciered mountains and deep fjords bordered by rich green pastureland, had named the country "Greenland," and was offering free land to those who wished to join him in his new home.

VIKING SHIPS CARRIED EXPLORERS AND VENTURERS AS FAR AS BAFFIN ISLAND, NEWFOUNDLAND AND THE GULF OF ST. LAWRENCE. THIS REPLICA CROSSED THE NORTH ATLANTIC IN 1991.

At a time when Iceland's limited pastures were becoming overcrowded, following a century of settlement, and cold temperatures had led to years of famine, it was not surprising that the following summer a flotilla of 25 ships set out to occupy the new country. Among the emigrants was Bjarni's father Herjolf, who took land at Herjolfsnes and became a leading citizen of the new country.

Bjarni convinced his small crew to continue their voyage to Greenland, but shortly after they had set off to the west they were struck by a storm that drove the ship far south of their intended route. When the storm finally ended, a fog descended on the ocean, and the ship drifted blindly for several days. Eventually the fog lifted, revealing a distant coast backed by low rolling hills—a country that Bjarni knew could not be the Greenland Eirik had described. Sailing northwards for two days, they encountered a coast that was flat and heavily forested and, after three more days, they came across the barren mountainous coast of an island. Here Bjarni decided he had travelled far enough to the north; turning eastwards, he sailed for four days and landed at his father's new home at the southern tip of Greenland.

The story of Bjarni Herjolfsson and his voyage of accidental discovery is preserved in an Icelandic saga, composed decades after the event and passed down through several generations as oral tradition before being preserved in writing. Such sagas were composed primarily to honour the histories and ancestral exploits of the families who supported the poets, and few provide accurate records of historical events or of geographical knowledge. However, the accuracy of this particular tale is supported by two sets of facts. Firstly, the *Groenlendinga Saga*—in which Bjarni's story is told—is devoted primarily to the history of Eirik the Red and his descendants, and yet it does not assign the discovery of the new lands to Eirik's son Leif, as does the other saga devoted to Norse adventures in the western Atlantic. Secondly, the tale is consistent with geography if we assume that the first land sighted by the storm-driven crew was the northeastern coast of Newfoundland, the flat forested land was the coast of central Labrador, and the barren mountainous land was the northern Labrador coast ending in the broad expanse of Hudson Strait. And if, as the saga recounts, Bjarni did turn offshore on reaching the northern tip of Labrador, and if, like other Viking sailors he was practising the navigational technique of sailing eastwards along a line of latitude by keeping the sun at a constant height, then within about four days he would indeed have struck Greenland within a few kilometres of his father's home at Herjolfsnes.

When Bjarni undertook his voyage, Iceland had been settled by Viking farmers for well over a century, and early Norse voyagers told of an Irish presence on the island before that time. Bjarni may not have been the first sailor to have been driven by storm far into the western Atlantic, but the existence of earlier discoveries is only hinted at by puzzling archaeological evidence and by vague allusions to a place called "Greater Ireland" in Norse historical traditions. At present, Bjarni Herjolfsson stands as the most likely candidate for the European who discovered Canada. His sightings led to a series of ventures by Icelanders and Norse Greenlanders over the following centuries.

When the first flotilla of immigrants arrived in Greenland during the summer of A.D. 986, the new country became home to a community of Norse farmers whose livelihood was based primarily on the milk and meat of sheep, goats and a few cattle. A small amount of grain could be grown on some farms, serviceable clothing could be spun from wool, and enough driftwood could be found to support the roofs of houses built from stone and turf. However, most of the materials and supplies needed to maintain a European way of life had to be imported from Iceland or Norway. In return, the Greenlanders traded woollen cloth, ivory tusks from walrus and narwhal, walrus skin (which could be cut into rope for ships' rigging), skins from polar bears and other animals and, occasionally, live bears and gyrfalcons. Hunting in order to obtain these trade materials was as important as farming to Greenland's economy, and hunters travelled widely as local animal populations were depleted. Acquiring trade goods became more important after A.D. 1000, when Greenland was Christianized, and especially after 1261, when the republic became a colony of Norway. By this time, in addition to the goods required for ongoing trade, ivory tusks and other valuables were required as payment for church tithes, crusade taxes and civil taxes, as well as for the equipment and vestments for about 15 parish churches, a bishop and his cathedral. Greenland may have been the most distant of Europe's colonies, but it was not an isolated backwater. Its population, estimated at between 2,000 and 5,000, maintained close ties with Europe: clothing recovered from frozen graveyards shows that Greenlanders followed the latest European fashions up until the death of the colonies around A.D. 1450. For almost five centuries, this small European society existed

within a few hundred kilometres of Canada's northeastern coast. It is inevitable that Norse sailors, hunters and explorers crossed the intervening sea many times, and it is likely that they made their presence felt in a variety of different ways.

The voyages that are most adequately documented in sagas were made within a few decades of Bjarni's initial venture, and most involved the children of Eirik the Red. Leif Eiriksson is reported to have purchased Bjarni's ship a few years after its first storm-driven voyage, and is credited with visiting and naming the lands that Bjarni had sighted: the barren mountainous country to the west of Greenland he called "Helluland" (Flatstone Land), a name that probably applied to both Baffin Island and the tundra coast of northern Labrador. The low-lying forested country to the south was named "Markland" (Forest Land), and can most probably be identified with central and southern Labrador. Leif named the most southerly country "Vinland" (Wine Land), due to the wild grapes that grew there. He and his crew spent the winter at a location that became known as "Leifsbudir" (Leif's booths), building houses and cutting a cargo of timber and grapevines to take home the following spring.

The next voyage was undertaken soon after by Leif's brother Thorvald, who borrowed Leif's ship and wintered at Leifsbudir. He spent the following summer exploring and, somewhere on the coast of Markland, had his first encounter with the country's Aboriginal inhabitants. A Norse attack led to a retaliatory raid in which Thorvald was killed by an arrow, and the remainder of the crew quickly returned to Greenland. A few years later, the sagas report, the most ambitious attempt

to settle in Vinland was led by an Icelandic couple, Thorfinn Karlsefni and his wife Gudrid. Karlsefni loaded his large merchant ship with 60 men, five women and an assortment of livestock, made an arrangement with Leif to use his houses, and passed two or three winters at Leifsbudir while exploring the surrounding country. For the first time, Native people arrived at Leifsbudir and proposed an exchange of animal furs for iron weapons; Karlsefni forbade his people to sell their weapons, but allowed them to trade other materials. After a second visit, which ended in violence and led to a further attack by Native peoples, Karlsefni decided to abandon his settlement and return to Greenland. In the words of the saga, "It now seemed plain to Karlsefni and his men that though the quality of the land was admirable, there would always be fear and strife dogging them there on account of those who already inhabited it." One further Vinland voyage is recorded for the following year, involving one Icelandic ship and a second under the command of Eirik the Red's daughter Freydis.

THE REMAINS OF A VIKING-AGE HOUSE ARE MARKED BY LOW RIDGES IN THE PASTURELAND NEAR THE VILLAGE OF L'ANSE AUX MEADOWS, AT THE NORTHERN TIP OF NEWFOUNDLAND.

She occupied the houses at Leifsbudir while the Icelanders built a new house for themselves, but the winter ended in a massacre of the Icelanders by Freydis and her men, and the settlement was finally abandoned.

The sailing directions and descriptions of Vinland that the sagas provide are vague and contradictory. Various enthusiasts have identified this country of large trees, grapevines and rivers teeming with salmon in places as diverse as Quebec, Cape Cod, Florida and Argentina. A Newfoundland location for Vinland has long been favoured by scholars, who rule

RECONSTRUCTION OF VIKING-AGE BUILDINGS AT L'ANSE AUX MEADOWS. TURF-WALLED STRUCTURES LIKE THESE WERE USED BY THE NORSE IN ICELAND AND GREENLAND.

out more southerly positions on the grounds that they were too distant to be reached by Greenlanders during the brief northern sailing season. This location gained support in 1960, when the Norwegian writer and adventurer Helge Ingstad discovered the archaeological remains of a small Viking-age European settlement at the northern tip of Newfoundland's Great Northern Peninsula. In a grassy pasture near the fishing village of L'Anse aux Meadows lay the severely eroded remains of three large dwellings built from turf in the Icelandic style, together with several smaller buildings, including a smithy. The small number of artifacts recovered indicates that the settlement was used for only a short period of time, but a soapstone spinning whorl suggests that women as well as men lived there, and a bronze clothing pin hints at the presence of wealthy or high-status individuals. Wood shavings and numerous iron ship rivets suggest that a ship was repaired there, and that perhaps a small amount of iron was smelted from local bog ore to make the rivets needed for this work.

Could the archaeological site at L'Anse aux Meadows have been the Leifsbudir described in the sagas? The coincidence would seem to be unlikely but, in recent years, a convincing argument has been made in favour of this identification. Sailing directions found in the sagas can be interpreted as supporting this conclusion, and the site has major advantages over other possible locations. At the extreme northern tip of Newfoundland, separated from the mainland by the narrow Strait of Belle Isle, L'Anse aux Meadows would have been a prominent and easy-to-find locale for ships following the Labrador coast southwards from Greenland. More importantly, it may have been the only area along the entire coast of Labrador, Newfoundland and the Gulf of St. Lawrence that was not occupied by a local Aboriginal population. The site is now interpreted as the remains of what may have been the only settlement that the Norse built during their southern ventures, a place used as a base for exploring and searching for timber, furs or other valuable goods along the coasts to the south, and as a wintering site for crews before they set out on the return trip to Greenland.

Archaeological findings at L'Anse aux Meadows included the shells of butternuts, which are not native to the area but grow on the coast of New Brunswick about 500 kilometres to the southwest, in forests that also support an abundance of wild grapes. Thus Leif Eiriksson's Vinland now seems most likely to have been the regions of temperate forest that line the southern and western coasts of the Gulf of St. Lawrence, from Cape Breton Island around to New Brunswick and Gaspé. The settlement at L'Anse aux Meadows would itself not have been in Vinland, but would have served as a way station and wintering base at the gateway to that country. It may well have been the Leifsbudir of the sagas.

When the Norse ventured to Markland and Vinland they encountered local non-European inhabitants for the first time in their western expansion across the Atlantic, and it's clear that the presence of these ancestors of the Newfoundland Beothuk, Labrador Innu and the Mi'kmaq peoples of the Gulf of St. Lawrence led to the Norse abandoning their intentions to settle Vinland. Unlike the Europeans who began crossing the Atlantic five centuries later, the Norse of the Viking age did not bear firearms and, more importantly, did not carry the diseases

that quickly laid waste to New World peoples after the sixteenth century. They simply could not compete—in numbers, weapons or knowledge of local conditions—against the resources that Native groups could bring to the skirmishes that quickly broke out between peoples from opposite sides of the world.

Although Norse attempts to settle Vinland probably ended before A.D. 1050, there is a historical record of a ship from Greenland visiting Markland three centuries later; voyages to obtain Labrador timber may have occurred throughout the occupation of Norse Greenland. Far to the north, more interesting developments appear to have been taking place on Baffin Island and in northern Labrador, the region known to the Norse as Helluland, and at this time occupied by a people known to the Inuit as Tuniit. Neither Indian nor Inuit, the ancestors of the Tuniit population seem to have immigrated from Siberia about 5,000 years ago and to have occupied Arctic Canada since that time. Ancestral Inuit, who moved eastwards from their Alaskan home a couple of centuries after the Norse arrived, described the Tuniit as a gentle and inoffensive people with primitive tools, who could easily be killed or chased away. Norse hunters and explorers on the Helluland coast may have found the small scattered groups of Tuniit less worrisome than their Indian neighbours of the forests to the south, and a few scraps of smelted metal recovered from Tuniit archaeological sites suggest that the

Norse may have traded their goods for ivory, furs and other valuable products that the Tuniit could provide. More interesting are numerous fragments of yarn spun from the fur of Arctic hare and other local animals: the yarn is identical to that spun from the wool of sheep and goats by women from Norse Greenland. The Aboriginal peoples of Arctic North America did not spin and weave cloth, but made superior clothing much more efficiently from tailored animal hides. Spinning is a very difficult technique and it would have taken close teaching and much practise to acquire the skills necessary to produce cordage of the quality found in Tuniit sites. The interpretation of this material, together with other specimens that resemble European technology and have been recovered from Tuniit sites, remains puzzling. However, it does suggest the possibility that the Norse and Tuniit were relatively familiar with one another, establishing significant contacts that may have lasted over a period of generations along the eastern coasts of Baffin Island and Labrador.

The arrival of the Inuit in the eastern Arctic during the twelfth or thirteenth century introduced another element into the history of the region. These were well-armed people with a tradition of warfare practised among the dense populations of Inuit and Indians in Alaska. Inuit oral history reports that the Tuniit were killed or displaced, and this accords well with archaeological evidence. In Norse accounts, the first mention of individuals likely to have been Inuit appears around A.D. 1260, and describes those encountered in far northwestern Greenland. Archaeological excavation of Inuit settlements from that area and time period have recovered large numbers of specimens that derive from contact with the Norse,

and these specimens were widely distributed across the Inuit trading network. It seems likely that trade—probably the exchange of ivory and other valuables in return for metal—developed between Norse and Inuit, although some of the metal found in Inuit settlements may have been obtained by raids on Norse ships or shore stations. A century later, when accounts first mention Inuit around the Norse settlements in southwestern Greenland, they usually refer to hostilities between the groups.

The Norse colonies in Greenland disappeared at some point during the fifteenth century, very shortly before European fishermen began crossing the Atlantic to fish for cod on the Grand Banks and to hunt whales along the coast of Labrador. The reason for their disappearance has never been fully understood, but it probably involved a number of factors. The fifteenth century was a time of colder weather in both Greenland and Iceland, bringing more frequent years in which farmers were unable to harvest enough hay to feed their livestock through the winters. Increasing sea ice interfered with contacts between Europe and the western colonies, as did the capture of Norwegian trade by the Hanseatic cities of the Baltic. When occasional ships did arrive from Europe, they may have carried contagious diseases against which the Norse Greenlanders would have had no more immunity than did the Aboriginal peoples of North America. Finally, the mere existence of Inuit neighbours may have caused anxiety among farmers who had never met non-Europeans. When the last family of Norse Greenlanders took ship for Iceland or Norway, probably around A.D. 1450, five centuries of European history along Canada's eastern coasts came to an end.

August 3, 1492

2. *Fishing the Newfoundland Banks*

August 3, 1492

As dawn broke over the tiny Spanish port of Palos, three small ships under the command of the Genoan navigator Cristoforo Colombo (whom we know as Christopher Columbus) set sail on the voyage that would bring the American continents to the attention of the Old World. When the crews returned almost nine months later, after visiting several Caribbean islands, their reports of gold, spices, cotton and friendly natives set off a new era in transatlantic navigation. But while Columbus was on his voyage of discovery, other European ships may well have been anchored over the fishing banks lying off the southern coast of Newfoundland.

THIS EIGHTEENTH-CENTURY ENGRAVING SHOWS THE PROCESS OF CUTTING, SALTING AND DRYING CODFISH FOR SHIPMENT TO EUROPEAN MARKETS.

Life aboard these small ships would have been quite different from the experience of explorers in the warm waters and pleasant islands of the subtropics. For days or weeks the world narrowed to a circle of fog and heaving grey water, the flap of fish sliding across the tilting deck, the creak of the ship's rigging and the cries of gulls scavenging the waste pitched overboard from the cutting table. Giant codfish, half the size and weight of a man, were pulled from the sea in an endless stream, hoisted over the rail, unhooked and dropped behind the fishermen. The hook, attached to a lead weight, was flung into the water and, before it had sunk to the seabed 40 metres below, was snatched by another fish identical to the last. The anchored ships swung slowly as the wind changed direction and, occasionally, the fog lifted fleetingly to reveal a distant green headland, a rocky finger extending from the island that marked the newly discovered fishing grounds.

The concentrations of animal life within these waters would prove them to be among the richest that the world has known. The cornucopia of sea creatures results from a unique geographical circumstance: the meeting of two broad rivers of sea water from very different parts of the world. From the south comes the Gulf Stream, a vein of warm salty tropical water over 100 kilometres wide; from the north, the Labrador current sweeps down from the Arctic, carrying the icebergs of Greenland in a stream of cold and oxygen-rich Arctic waters. The two oceanic rivers collide over an immense undersea plain extending southeastwards from Newfoundland, bringing together all of the conditions needed to spawn myriad tiny creatures and the ascending chain of animal life feeding on them. And, for thousands of years, the marine life of the

THIS MAP DATES TO 1492, AND MAY HAVE BELONGED TO CHRISTOPHER COLUMBUS. THE RED ARROW POINTS TO A GROUP OF ISLANDS FAR TO THE WEST OF IRELAND, AND NORTHWEST OF THE AZORES. IT MAY REPRESENT NEWFOUNDLAND, AND COULD BE EVIDENCE OF EARLY PORTUGUESE DISCOVERY OF THE ISLAND.

Grand Banks had another advantage: it thrived in a part of the world where humans had not developed the technology required to exploit it. Until the 1400s, the codfish that swam at the top of the local food chain lived undisturbed by hooks and nets. But a great change was coming.

The ships' crews who may have anchored off Newfoundland's southeastern coast in 1492 spoke either English (in the soft accents of the West Country port of Bristol), or Portuguese. The fishermen and sailors of England and Portugal had explored westwards across the Atlantic for several generations, the English fishing in Icelandic waters since about 1410 and the Portuguese discovering the mid-Atlantic Azores island group during the 1430s. During the last decades of the fifteenth century, a few historical accounts hint at visits to a mysterious distant island, which began to appear on Portuguese maps under various names: Brasil, Antillia or Illa Verde (Green Island—perhaps a reminder of Greenland). On maps drawn in the 1480s and 1490s, this island was placed far to the southwest of Iceland and at about the same latitude as Ireland. At least occasional fishing ships carrying supplies of salt were heading westwards on long voyages well to the west of Ireland.

The 1497 voyage of exploration made by the Venetian Giovanni Caboto (John Cabot) appears to have taken him directly to this area, where he discovered an island that he claimed for the King of England. When he reported his discovery, a knowledgeable English merchant wrote to Christopher Columbus that Cabot's "Newe Found Islande" had been known for some time to sailors from Bristol. Some historians now suspect that Cabot may have been following in the wake of secretive fishermen, for whom Newfoundland was not a destination but, rather, a marker for the valuable cod fishery on its offshore banks.

For a Christian European population whose religious calendar required abstinence from meat on three or more days of the week, marine fishing had become an important industry. The fishery had begun in medieval times off the coasts of Northern Europe, where fishermen developed the techniques of handlining for cod and drying the fish for export to southern markets. By the fifteenth century, the Icelandic banks were producing much of Europe's dried codfish, but by the 1470s, English fishing was being outlawed by the Icelandic authorities. Only a generation earlier Norse farmers still lived in Greenland, and as late as 1347 a voyage to Labrador was recorded in an Icelandic annal. It is easy to imagine that memories of a land to the west—and perhaps of seas teeming with codfish—were still preserved among Icelandic seafarers, and that this knowledge could have been passed on to the English fishermen with whom they did business. The early English interest in the lands of the northwestern Atlantic may have been stimulated by geographical knowledge acquired by the Norse, and might be seen as a natural continuation of five centuries of Norse exploration and use of the region.

Despite England's official 1497 claim of the Newe Found Islande, by the early 1500s English fishermen were far outnumbered by those from Brittany and elsewhere on the coasts of France, Spain and Portugal. A leading role was played by the Portuguese, to whom the Pope had assigned all newly

BY 1502 THIS PORTUGUESE MAP SHOWS A WOODED ISLAND IN THE WESTERN ATLANTIC.
WHEN COMPARED TO IRELAND AND GREENLAND, IT SPANS THE LATITUDES OF
NEWFOUNDLAND AND LABRADOR, AND IS MARKED "LAND OF THE KING OF PORTUGAL."

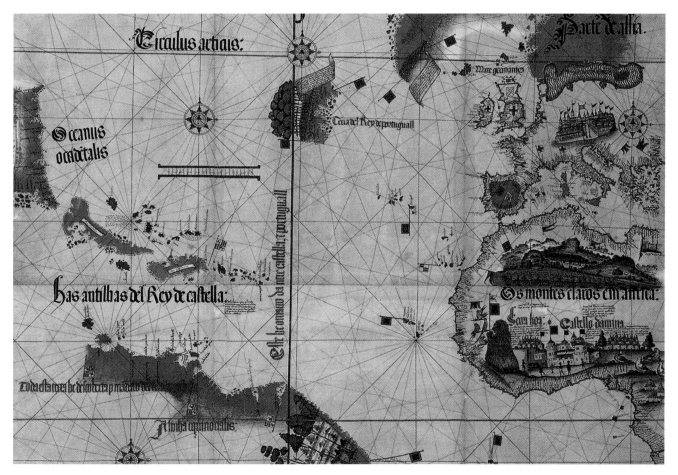

discovered lands lying east of about the fiftieth meridian. At a time when longitude could be estimated only vaguely, this was interpreted as including Cape Breton Island, Newfoundland, Greenland and Brazil. The first recorded European settlement in North America was established, probably as a shore station for drying fish, around 1520 by the Portuguese João Alvarez Fagundes, somewhere on the eastern coast of Cape Breton Island. The colony lasted long enough for its members to learn several local Mi'kmaq place names, which appear on European maps of the time, but it seems to have been abandoned after a few years in the face of local hostilities.

Throughout most of the 1500s, the European fishermen continued to pay little attention to the land alongside the fishing grounds. Many of them packed their fish in salt and returned to Europe as soon as they had gathered a full cargo; if they went ashore at all, it was only to obtain firewood and drinking water from a handy cove. Others preserved the fish by drying, a process in which the fish were split, lightly salted and laid out on the gravel or shingle of a beach, turned occasionally, stacked and covered when it rained, and stowed aboard ship when they had acquired the weight and texture of light wood. This dried product was known as "stockfish," a food that will not spoil for several years and is easily reconstituted by soaking in water. It soon became a staple throughout Western Europe, a basic ingredient in several delicious cuisines, and North America's first major export to the world.

The making of stockfish required several weeks ashore and, throughout the 1500s, European shore crews scattered to

suitable beaches and harbours adjacent to the fishing banks. To manage the competition for good harbours and drying beaches, the fishermen had a general agreement that the captain of the first ship to arrive in a harbour was the "admiral" of the locality for the summer, allocating space and settling disputes between later arrivals. The shore crews built temporary shelters, and in harbours that had no sand or gravel beach they constructed flakes—long table-like structures covered with light sticks and branches on which the drying fish were laid. It is possible that more permanent structures were built in a few especially favoured harbours, but the Portuguese settlement established on Cape Breton Island in the 1520s may have been unique in attempting year-round occupation during this early period.

It was into this society of scattered shore crews, fishing admirals and hundreds of fishing ships dispersed across the banks that Sir Humphrey Gilbert sailed in August 1583. Entering the magnificent harbour of St. John's, he found 36 vessels from France, Portugal, Spain and England. In the presence of their crews, he renewed Cabot's claim of English sovereignty over the Newe Found Islande, a matter that was not contested and was probably of little interest to the assembled fishermen as long as it did not interfere with their rights to fish the offshore waters. The episode did, however, lay the foundation for centuries of political negotiation and occasional warfare over competing rights to the use of these coasts.

Spanish and Portuguese interests in the fishing grounds decreased abruptly only five years later, when a significant number of ships from Spain and Portugal were lost in the debacle of the Spanish Armada. The next two centuries saw power shifting between the English and French, and the eventual designation of English and French regions of coast. However, these agreements did not extend to the offshore banks and their rich stocks of fish, a resource that remained free for all. The competing claims established by the fishermen of the 1400s and 1500s eventually played out in the tragedy that destroyed the cod stocks of the Newfoundland banks during the 1980s and 1990s. Until the 1970s the Portuguese White Fleet had been an attractive feature of St. John's harbour during autumn storms. When the wind dropped, the white-hulled ships laden with stacks of dories disappeared back to the fishing banks, where their crews handlined cod in much the way that their ancestors had done almost five centuries before. From Newfoundland and Nova Scotia harbours, inshore fishermen continued to catch cod by handlining, and to net them in elaborate coastal traps. Neither technique could make significant inroads on the cod populations. More ominous were the huge industrial trawlers that steamed to the fishing banks year-round from ports across Europe, exercising their ancient and historical rights to this common resource. Twentieth-century trawler technology rapidly destroyed the cod fishery and most other valued species living on the Grand Banks, but the previous five centuries of history provided the political conditions that made this destruction possible.

Circulus arcticus.

Occanus occidentalis

Has antilhas del Rey de castella.

December 24, 1584

3. The Basque Whale Fishery

December 24, 1584

The whaler Joanes de Echaniz lay dying in the dark hold of the ship. It was midnight as he slowly dictated his will to the surgeon, who had written many such documents and was familiar with the legal wording. The ship's master and two whalers witnessed the signing of the will; de Echaniz's other shipmates were either working ashore or were too exhausted from the day's labour to sit up with the dying man. He specified that several small donations were to be made for candles, and requested masses to be said at the parish church of Saint Nicholas in Orio, his hometown and that of his wife and daughter, to whom he left the remainder of his possessions. The small Spanish town of Orio, in the pleasant Basque country nestled in the fertile plain between the High Pyrenees and the Bay of Biscay, was far from Terra Nova, where the dying whaler found himself on this winter night.

Beyond the thick oak hull of the whaling ship, the black water glistened in the light of fires from the nearby shore. The flames illuminated clouds of smoke torn by the wind, the figures of men stirring huge cauldrons, and others working with cutting spades atop the carcass of a whale floating alongside the beach. The work continued day and night so that a full cargo of whale oil could be collected and loaded before the water froze and trapped the ships on this desolate and hostile coast. Dawn would reveal the rocky shores of the bay in which the ship was anchored, surrounded by a forest of spruce trees rising to barren hills drifted with early winter snow. Beyond the harbour entrance lay the open water of the Grand Bay, an area known today as the Strait of Belle Isle and the northern Gulf of St. Lawrence. Over a period of more than 40 years, between about 1540 and 1585, this region saw the establishment of the first European industrial enterprise in North America, an activity that usually involved more than a thousand men working from harbours along Labrador's southern coast and the adjacent north shore region of the Gulf.

The whale fishery in the Grand Bay developed in response to the need for oil, a resource that was essential to the growing European populations of the sixteenth century. Oil was a basic ingredient in foods, soaps and medicines, and was used in the manufacture of cloth and leather goods; it lubricated the wooden machinery of early industries, and lighted the homes and businesses of cities. Olive oil had traditionally supplied the needs of southern countries, but vegetable oils and the oils rendered from the fat of domestic animals were clearly insufficient for the expanding communities of Northern and Western Europe. Whale oil was an excellent alternative and,

since late medieval times, had been a source of wealth for the Basque communities that had developed techniques and skills for hunting the large whales of the Bay of Biscay. By the sixteenth century, whale oil was a valuable commodity in a Europe that had come to depend on the substance.

The Basques had begun whaling in small boats launched from the shores of the Bay of Biscay, but this practice diminished during the fifteenth century as whales became scarce or moved into safer offshore waters. Hunters responded by using sea-going ships from which to launch their hunting boats in the open ocean, and became expert offshore mariners. The first Basques to sail as far as Newfoundland waters were not whalers, but cod fishermen drawn by the reports of teeming schools of cod sighted by explorers during the 1490s. By 1520, the Basques were fishing among their Breton neighbours on Newfoundland banks, and they may have been the first to venture northwards into the Strait of Belle Isle, where they could observe the fall migration of whales through the area. By 1540, Basque ships in the Grand Bay were engaged in three trades: codfishing, whaling and privateering. For the next 40 years, up to 20 whaling ships were anchored each summer in several small harbours along a 100-kilometre segment of the Labrador coast.

Transatlantic whaling was an expensive business, requiring skills in both financing and outfitting an expedition, in addition to the expertise needed for killing whales. Documents preserved in Spanish and French archives reveal complex financial transactions involving the owner of a ship, the outfitters who organized the undertaking and the insurers who underwrote the voyage. The owner (who sometimes also served as captain) supplied a ship that was ready to sail, together with a boatswain, carpenter, caulker, gunner and other skilled sailors, as well as sufficient cannons, swivel guns and gunpowder to protect the ship. The outfitters recruited the remainder of the crew, provided the supplies for the voyage, and the equipment for hunting whales and rendering their oil. The crews ranged from 50 to over 100 men, depending on the size of the ship; each crewman provided his own clothing for work in the cold wet conditions of Labrador, and an arquebus or crossbow to help defend the ship from attack. Profits from the voyages, and the crew's wages, were distributed as shares in the cargo of oil: the ship's owner seems usually to have received about 25 per cent of the profits from the venture, the crew about 30 per cent, and the syndicate of outfitters divided the remainder among themselves.

A successful voyage could be extremely profitable; the recorded revenue from one cargo of whale oil was approximately equal to the value of two new galleons. The share that was added to the estate of Joanes de Echaniz at the time of his death on the Labrador coast was approximately 80 times the price brought by the sale of his workboots to another whaler, and 20 times the price paid for his arquebus and sword. In terms of modern prices, we might estimate the share owed to this common whaler at the end of the hunting season as being worth somewhere between $10,000 and $20,000: a somewhat meagre return for nine months of hard and dangerous work, but sufficient to attract men from small peasant villages of the Basque country to undergo the hazards and privations of a voyage to the Grand Bay.

Whaling ships generally set sail in early summer, arriving after a transatlantic passage that often took more than two months. A harbour was selected close to the expected route of whales moving through the area, and shore facilities were built or refurbished. Permanent tryworks were soon constructed in most of the better harbours along the Labrador shore of the Grand Bay. Tryworks were massive stone platforms containing up to five fireboxes lined with clay and built to support copper cauldrons a metre or more in diameter. A wooden working deck was constructed from which the cauldrons could be filled, stirred and emptied and, in some cases, the deck was roofed with a wooden frame covered by ceramic tiles. Other shore facilities might include a cooper's shop, where the skilled tradesmen assembled the barrels that were crucial to storing whale oil for the journey home. Individual crewmen seem to have lived aboard ship, or built themselves small and primitive shelters scattered across the nearby hillsides.

During the whaling season, the ships were permanently anchored off the tryworks, their sterns moored to the shore by heavy ropes. The actual hunting was done by parties of six or eight men rowing narrow canoe-like shallops, several of which were carried on each ship. The quarry was slow-swimming and relatively docile right whales, which could be taken from such boats. When a whale was spotted, the crew gave chase, trying to approach the animal as quietly as possible and from the back, where they could not be seen. When the boat was within a few metres of the whale, a harpooner in the bow speared it with a barbed iron harpoon attached to a rope more than 300 metres long. The wounded animal dived or swam away in panic, while the rope, coiled in the boat, ran out so quickly that it smoked. The other end of the rope was tied to the boat, and if the whale took the entire rope, the crew had to decide whether to cut the line or be dragged along the surface in a dangerous manoeuvre that came to be known among nineteenth-century whalers as a "Nantucket sleighride." When the whale eventually tired, it was killed with long lances and towed to harbour, a task that usually involved two or more boats and several hours of exhausting work.

Although the hunt was the most dangerous work on a whaling voyage, the most arduous task was that of stripping the blubber and rendering it to oil. The thick sheets of fat were removed from the whale with razor-edged cutting spades, and hauled to the cooking platform with iron hooks. Here, they were minced into small pieces and boiled in cauldrons over fires fuelled with wood and the fritters left over from the last rendering. The oil was eventually ladled out, cooled in troughs or in old whaleboats half-filled with water, and stored

THIS IMAGINATIVE EARLY ENGRAVING DEPICTS THE HUNTING AND PROCESSING OF WHALES DURING THE SIXTEENTH CENTURY.

ARTIST'S RECONSTRUCTION OF THE WHALE-PROCESSING INDUSTRY AT RED BAY.

in barrels that were rowed out to the ship and stacked in the hold for transport to the markets of Europe.

Transatlantic shipping of whale oil was subject not only to the usual hazards of storm and wave but also to the piracy and privateering that was rampant on sixteenth-century oceans. All whaling ships were well armed, either to repel an attack or to carry one out. In the early years, when France and Spain were at war, Basques from both sides of the border hijacked one another's ships. When religious wars flared across Europe during the later sixteenth century, the whalers carried their hostilities across the ocean: Basques were pitted against Protestants from France, England and the Netherlands. Cargoes of whale oil and dried cod were sufficiently valuable to attract the same pirates who looted treasure ships from New Spain, emphasizing the importance of these commodities in early post-medieval Europe. Some historians have estimated that the oil and fish removed from Newfoundland waters during the sixteenth century were of greater value than the Peruvian gold and Mexican silver amassed by Spanish conquistadors. The sudden influx of precious metals into Europe has been credited with establishing the financial base from which the later Industrial Revolution was to arise. It seems likely that the fats and protein imported from Eastern Canada nourished the population that would be needed to undertake that revolution.

Whaling in the Grand Bay came to an end during the 1580s, but the reason for its demise is unclear. Some have suggested that the increasing presence of hostile Inuit in southern Labrador during the late sixteenth century may have posed a problem for the Basques. The Aboriginal peoples occupying the area when the Basques arrived were ancestral to the Innu peoples of the Labrador forests, and archaeological finds suggest that Innu visited the Basque establishments—some may even have been employed in the heavy onshore work of the whaling industry. The Inuit, in contrast, were newcomers who had arrived in the eastern Arctic from ancestral homes in Alaska, and were drawn south along the Labrador coast by the prospect of trading with the Europeans who were fishing and whaling in the area. The Inuit were the pre-eminent whalers of North America, just as the Basques excelled at whaling in Europe. During nineteenth-century whaling ventures in Arctic Canada, Inuit were frequently employed as boatmen and harpooners, or contracted to hunt whales with their own crews and equipment. Inuit skills in whaling may have led to similar employment in the Grand Bay, and although the Inuit also pilfered the shore facilities when the Basques returned to Europe, relations between the two peoples may not have been limited to hostilities.

It is also possible that Basque whaling may have been sufficiently intense that it reduced the populations of whales in the northwestern Atlantic, as appears to have happened earlier in the Bay of Biscay and would happen during the following century in Spitsbergen waters. But a historical event was probably of greater significance in the sudden decline of Grand Bay whaling: the defeat of the Spanish Armada that was sent against England during the summer of 1588. Many of the Basque galleons that were lost in this disastrous endeavour had been employed in the whale fishery. The financial loss to owners, and the scarcity of ships needed to revive the enterprise, may have been the primary cause for the termination of Grand Bay whaling.

When a new whale fishery was established a few decades later, it was focused on the whale stocks in Arctic waters off Spitsbergen. This undertaking was in the hands of the Dutch and English, but they employed Basque boatmen and harpooners on their first ventures in order to learn the trade. When the whales of the Barents Sea were wiped out, the increasingly efficient whale industry turned first to Greenland waters, and then to Arctic North America. The great whales of northern waters were saved from near extinction only by the discovery, early in the twentieth century, that crude oil pumped from the ground could be distilled into inexpensive products that substituted for the whale oil used previously. Less fortunate are the whale stocks of Antarctic waters, which survived the oil boom through sheer inaccessibility, but are now subject to industrial hunting to feed populations hungry for their meat. If history is a guide, their long-term survival seems unlikely.

The Basque fishery in the Grand Bay remained a largely forgotten episode in Canadian history until it was recently brought to light by a combination of archaeology in Labrador and research in the small municipal archives of Basque country. Here were discovered the contracts, insurance undertakings and lawsuits that could be fitted together to build a picture of Canada's first industrial enterprise. More poignant documents were also found here, including testaments written at the request of whalers like

Joanes de Echaniz, who died on Christmas Eve, longing for family and home, unable to toil any longer in this cold land at the end of the world.

4. The Battle at Carillon

May 1660

May is high-water season on the Ottawa River. Fed by the melting snowpack in the spruce forests south of Hudson Bay, the river slides southwards into warmer regions where the snow has long disappeared and the hardwood forests are brilliant with flowers and newly unfurled leaves. The river is icy, fast and dangerous, tumbling through canyons or flowing widely and swiftly between banks lined with submerged trees and bushes. This is also blackfly season on the lower Ottawa, the few weeks in spring when hot sunny days spawn masses of biting insects from the frigid water. Today, intrepid rafters and kayakers use this time to play in the river's rapids, while other boaters wait ashore for the water to warm, the flies to disappear and the currents to become more predictable.

CHAMPLAIN'S 1609 ATTACK ON THE MOHAWK SET THE STAGE FOR A CONTINUING WAR BETWEEN THE IROQUOIS WHO LIVED SOUTH OF THE ST. LAWRENCE RIVER, AND THE FRENCH WITH THEIR HURON AND ALGONQUIN ALLIES, LIVING IN WHAT IS NOW QUEBEC AND ONTARIO.

A century ago, this season saw the greatest use of the river, as spring floods carried rafts of timber from northern logging camps to ships waiting on the St. Lawrence River. Three centuries before that, the high waters in May carried the canoes of Aboriginal hunters and traders, transporting beaver pelts hunted during the winter to the trading posts on the St. Lawrence and Hudson Rivers to the south.

Furs were the magnet that drew Europeans into northern North America, and the sale of furs enticed Native merchants to the ships and stores of the early European venturers. When two alien societies encounter one another, the most favourable outcomes probably occur when each has easy access to a product that the other considers of great value. This was the fortunate situation in Eastern Canada during the early centuries of contact, when the exchange of beaver pelts obtained by Aboriginal peoples for iron hatchets and knives, brass kettles, muskets and gunpowder provided by Europeans proved profitable to both sides. The centuries of mutual trade that resulted from this balance of interests produced circumstances far different from those that arose in more southerly regions of the continent. The Indigenous peoples of southeastern North America had little of value to arriving Europeans, and were seen merely as impediments to settlement. The gold and silver controlled by the Native empires of Mexico and Peru were of such great value as to invite plunder rather than trade. The mutually profitable early Canadian fur trade did, however, spawn its own share of violence and tragedy.

The trade began from the ships of sixteenth-century cod fishermen and whalers but, early in the next century, onshore stations began to be established for buying furs. French trading posts began a steady progression up the St. Lawrence: Quebec City was established by Champlain in 1608, Trois-Rivières in 1635, and Ville-Marie on Île-de-Montréal in 1642. The Native farming people whom Jacques Cartier had met there a century before had long disappeared, likely victims of warfare with their Iroquois relatives who fought for access to the lucrative shipboard trade in the Gulf of St. Lawrence, and of epidemics caught from sailors on those same ships. The St. Lawrence was now a no man's land between the peoples of the northern forests, hunters who spoke Algonquin languages and traded with the French, and the Iroquois farmers to the south, who traded with the Dutch and later the English on the Hudson River.

Beavers were quickly eradicated from the St. Lawrence River Valley, and trade soon depended on the high-quality furs that came instead from the northern forests. For the first half of the 1600s, much of this trade was in the hands of the Hurons, a farming people related to the Iroquois, who occupied what is now southern Ontario and whose commercial networks extended far north of the Great Lakes. The most direct canoe route from Huron country to the trading posts on the St. Lawrence River began in northeastern Georgian Bay, crossed to the upper Ottawa River and then descended the river to the French settlements. Each spring, fleets of canoes laden with furs were carried south on the swollen river, returning with ironware, guns and gunpowder later in the season when the current had slackened. However, the greatest danger on the Ottawa came not from spring floods but from encounters with hostile Iroquois who also needed

ARTIST'S CONCEPTION OF VILLE-MARIE ABOUT THE TIME OF DOLLARD'S ADVENTURE.

beaver pelts from the north in order to continue trading with the Dutch and English.

By 1650, the Iroquois had invaded the Huron homeland around southern Georgian Bay, where a nation already weakened by epidemics was finally dispersed, its remaining members fleeing to what is now the province of Quebec or to the western Great Lakes. For the following decades, the lower regions of the Ottawa River were in Iroquois hands. Huron and Algonquin traders bringing furs to the French posts rarely chanced the Ottawa, preferring the longer and more difficult routes along the turbulent rivers flowing through the Laurentian highlands of central Quebec. The Ottawa was now used primarily by Iroquois traders freighting cargoes of furs obtained from the upper Great Lakes, bypassing the French posts of the St. Lawrence to sell to their Dutch and English allies on the Hudson River and along the New England coast.

May 1660 saw an event on the lower Ottawa that was to have great significance in Canadian history. No records of the weather survive, but we can imagine the days of unexpected warmth, the ice-cold river tugging at trees along its flooded banks, the forest floor covered with drifts of white trilliums, and the warm air filled with blackflies. The incident was precipitated by Adam Dollard des Ormeaux, a 25-year-old soldier recently arrived from France and now an officer of the garrison protecting the village of Ville-Marie. The tiny settlement was centred around a wooden fort and trading warehouse, chapel, hospital and a few shops clustered along the shore where Old Montréal now stands. The surrounding forest was broken by a few outlying farmsteads that had been cleared during the

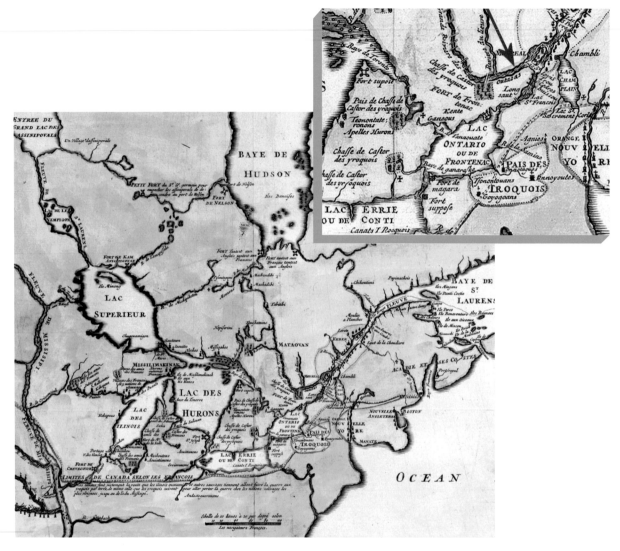

previous decade, and the entire population numbered less than 400 people. During the previous winter there had been the usual rumours of a planned Iroquois attack on Ville-Marie, the most exposed and poorly defended of the French settlements. It is unclear how these rumours related to the venture now planned by Dollard and a few young companions, but the few shreds of direct evidence seem to suggest that the primary motive behind their scheme was personal gain and glory.

Whatever the case, in late April Dollard and 16 other young Frenchmen set off in canoes to ambush the Iroquois fur brigades descending the Ottawa. At some point they joined forces with a party of 40 Hurons and four Algonquins who had arrived in Ville-Marie with a similar plan. Between the strong current and the French party's lack of experience in river travel, they spent ten days struggling upstream to the western end of Île-de-Montréal, crossing Lac des Deux-

A FRENCH MAP RECORDS THE EXTENT OF THE FUR TRADE IN EASTERN CANADA, A FEW DECADES AFTER THE TIME OF DOLLARD AND RADISSON. THE RED ARROW ON THE INSET POINTS TO THE SITE OF DOLLARD'S BATTLE.

montagnes and entering the lower course of the Ottawa near the present community of Oka—a route that commuters now traverse in 30 minutes in light traffic. Their ambush was to take place at the first rapids on the Ottawa, and here they set up camp in a small log stockade that had been built by an Algonquin party the previous year. Scattered groups of Iroquois hunters and traders travelling downstream in canoes loaded with furs, their ammunition exhausted during the winter's hunt, should not have posed a threat for this well-armed force. For decades the Iroquois had set similar traps on the Ottawa; now masters of the river, they would never have envisioned themselves becoming victims of an ambush.

What was planned—and what should have occurred—was another of the countless unrecorded skirmishes that scarred the history of the early fur trade, resulting in a few men dead or chased into the forest, and a cargo of furs changing hands. Instead, Dollard's party had barely arrived when they found themselves facing a fleet of canoes carrying about 200 Iroquois soldiers. After an initial volley, a truce was arranged but, although neither side seems to have had much heart for a fight, a series of badly timed actions escalated the melee into a full-scale battle. The Iroquois laid siege to the makeshift fort, and sporadic scuffles continued for a few days until several hundred additional Iroquois arrived to participate in the eventual victory. Most of the Hurons inside the fort deserted to their Iroquois relatives and, on the seventh or eighth day, the starving defenders were overwhelmed. The final blow came when the French tried to throw a gunpowder keg with lighted fuse over the palisade, which fell back into the fort and exploded. All but four of the French were killed; these

survivors were taken prisoner to meet soldiers' deaths by torture in various Iroquois villages. The Iroquois, according to a statement that they later reported to the Dutch, counted 14 dead and another 19 wounded.

Eight days after the battle, the scene was discovered by another party of historical personages: Pierre-Esprit Radisson and his brother-in-law Médard Chouart, Sieur des Groseilliers. The traders were returning from a year-long voyage made to the country between Lakes Michigan and Superior in an attempt to revive the trade interrupted by the dispersal of the Hurons. They were accompanied by a large party of Indians from the upper Great Lakes, and by a rich cargo of furs. Some historians have suggested that Dollard may have been planning to clear the river of Iroquois in expectation of the arrival of this valuable consignment, but this explanation has never been convincing. Nor has the interpretation that he and his companions were bent on sacrificing themselves to save Ville-Marie from an Iroquois attack. In order to accomplish the latter objective, rather than travelling westwards to the Ottawa, the party of young Frenchmen would have gone eastwards to the Richelieu River, the route by which Iroquois attackers could be expected to travel from their homeland in what is now New York State.

It has never been clear why a large party of well-armed Iroquois were on the lower Ottawa that spring; the location was clearly out of their way if they had planned to attack a French settlement. However, given the effectiveness of communication along the canoe routes of the day, it seems quite possible that they had been attracted by news of the large shipment of furs expected with the French explorers, and were planning the same sort of trap intended by Dollard for Iroquois merchants. Had the Iroquois ambush taken place, the travellers would have been easily overwhelmed, their furs sold in Albany, and Radisson and des Groseilliers would never have been heard of again. After the successful siege of Dollard's fort, however, the Iroquois had had their fill of spring warfare. Most of them had returned to their villages when Radisson's brigade arrived; the remainder, outnumbered and low on ammunition, quickly fled downriver. The travellers from the upper Great Lakes passed safely downstream and reached French territory. Years later, Radisson wrote in his journal that the Dollard incident—which he described as a simple attempt at plundering Iroquois traders—had undoubtedly saved his own life and the lives of his companions. The consequences were to have a significant effect on Canadian history.

When they arrived in Quebec City, Radisson and des Groseilliers were thrown in jail and had their furs confiscated for trading without a licence issued by the French authorities. Angry and disillusioned, the explorers turned to the English. While on Lake Superior they had learned of a canoe route to salt water in the north; indeed, Radisson even claimed that they had made a quick (and almost certainly fictitious) visit to the northern sea. The explorers now suggested that the English might profitably back a scheme to exploit northern furs by way of Hudson Bay. Within a decade, and under Radisson's guidance, the Hudson's Bay Company was establishing trading posts around the bay of that name, and claiming ownership of all territories draining into its waters.

For three centuries, church historians in French Canada depicted Adam Dollard des Ormeaux and his companions as martyrs, young men who had given their lives to save the tiny French outpost from which Montréal would later grow. Since then, Dollard's reputation has withered under the pens of more recent historians who portray him—perhaps more accurately—as a simple warrior of the fur trade. However, Pierre-Esprit Radisson appreciated that if Dollard and his companions had not acted as they did, then his own party would probably have been destroyed in an ambush at the rapids on the Ottawa. Radisson's safe passage allowed him to carry furs to Quebec City, to have them confiscated and, consequently, to show the English how to exploit the vast fur resources of the northern forests. Inadvertently, Dollard had laid the foundations for the eventual English claim to all of Central and Western Canada.

5. New France

August 1749

During the first week of August, Pehr Kalm travelled by river from Montréal to Quebec City. The young Swedish scientist had come to North America to search for native plants that could benefit Northern European agriculture, and had recently arrived in Canada from New York by way of the Hudson River. For the past ten days the traveller had enjoyed the hospitality of Montréal society, a round of visits and dinners, and day trips into the surrounding countryside. But now the small lively city was far behind him, and he found himself in a boat rowed by 10 soldiers, on a broad and quiet river flowing between endlessly flat landscapes. The boat moved slowly through four hot and cloudy days, while Kalm passed the time recording the scenery in his journal: low riverbanks, trees and other plants that appealed to his botanical interests, and human settlement.

THIS VIEW OF EIGHTEENTH-CENTURY QUEBEC FROM ACROSS THE ST. LAWRENCE RIVER SHOWS THE CITY MUCH AS IT WAS SEEN BY PEHR KALM.

On the banks of the river he noted an almost unbroken string of white farmhouses, interrupted occasionally by a large wayside cross, the slow-turning vanes of a stone windmill and, every few kilometres, a church steeple. He described the riverbanks as one continuous village running from Montréal to Quebec City, a pleasant community where cattle strolled down to drink from the river, and his boatmen bantered with farmers working in the fields. This pastoral landscape between Montréal and Quebec City was also the heartland of French America, the core of a trading empire that stretched from Newfoundland to Lake Superior and south to the Gulf of Mexico.

New France was almost 150 years old, and had grown from a scattering of fur-trading outposts along the St. Lawrence River into a society of 60,000 people. Over 2,000 now lived within Montréal's fortifications, and the town had become the hub of the fur trade that continued to serve as the economic engine of the colony. Quebec City had 5,000 inhabitants, and was surrounded by recently completed stone fortifications mounting over 200 cannons. Most of the arable terrain along the river between these two centres was now cultivated by farming families, the people who had become known as "habitants" and who now numbered more than 50,000.

Arriving in Quebec City, Kalm was invited to dinner by the Governor General of the colony, an amateur scientist whose intelligence and achievements he praised highly. This encounter gave Kalm access to all levels of society, and in his journal he enthusiastically described those whom he met. The Quebec City that he saw boasted impressive stone buildings in landscaped grounds, bordered by military fortifications that made use of the high bluffs overlooking the river. Visitors compared the town to a French provincial capital and, in fact, Quebec City was the administrative centre of New France. Two of its major buildings were homes to those who ruled the colony in the name of the King of France: the Governor General, who was responsible for military matters, and the Intendant, who directed the financial and judicial aspects of administration. A sizeable contingent of soldiers was garrisoned in the city, some of them for local defence and others in transit to more distant regions of the colony.

Quebec City was also the seat of the Bishop of New France, and in addition to the cathedral it had seven churches, a Jesuit college and a small seminary, as well as four convents whose nuns operated a hospital, a home for the aged and infirm, and two schools. In the Lower Town, on the sloping riverbank beneath the fortifications, merchants and artisans occupied a crowded quarter of tall and narrow houses on winding streets. In August, the docks were crowded with merchant ships that had left Europe in the late spring to avoid the icebergs of Newfoundland waters. Their consignments of metal and glassware, wine, brandy, guns and ammunition for the fur trade, as well as the latest fashions in European clothing, supplied all of North America's French settlements. Cargoes of furs and dried fish destined for France, as well as flour and biscuits for the military garrison at Louisbourg, were quickly loaded so that the return voyage could be completed before the onset of autumn's storms. The city's partly cobbled streets were alive with horse-drawn calèches, freight carts pulled by oxen, and people from all levels of society going about their business.

Quebec City may have resembled a French city in some ways, but a visitor from France would have found life there quite different from that at home. In theory, New France had inherited the Old World's class-based society composed of nobility, clergy and merchants, along with a broad class of commoners including peasants, artisans and servants. However, this system had barely survived the Atlantic crossing to the New World, and had lost much of its power to hold individuals to their place within its rigid stratification. One major blow was the absence in the new colony of a hereditary nobility based on ancient tenure of immense landholdings. For over a century, the French government had granted large holdings along the St. Lawrence to "seigneurs" who could lease portions of their land to peasant tenants, thus establishing a system resembling that of rural France. However, few of the seigneurs were of the French nobility: most were merchants and entrepreneurs who had convinced the government that they could attract peasant tenants and develop the agricultural base of the colony. In doing so, they found that, compared to the overcrowded peasantry of rural France, these tenants—or habitants—demanded much lower rents and much greater security of tenure.

Pehr Kalm described the habitants as universally hospitable, generous and well-spoken in comparison with European peasants. The difference was probably due to the fact that, in all but theory, these were independent landowners rather than landless farmers enmeshed in a system of insecurity and suspicion that repressed any hope of change. Most of the habitants' farms were large enough to meet their needs, rental obligations to the seigneur were not usually onerous, taxes were far lower than in France, and even the church tithe was half that paid by French peasants. The majority of habitants also had means of escaping the farm in order to make good money in other branches of the economy. For those in the vicinity of Quebec City, the cod fishery in the St. Lawrence estuary provided seasonal employment. Almost 500 young men from farms around Montréal worked in the fur trade. Most of these were canoemen who set off each summer, paddling and carrying the huge canoes that freighted supplies to isolated settlements such as Detroit or to the Lake Superior and upper Mississippi Valley posts, returning in late summer or the following spring with cargoes of furs for the export market.

Throughout its history, the fur trade provided the basis for the economy and indeed the existence of New France. Furs dominated the colony's exports, even when an overwhelming proportion of the population was engaged in farming. The extent of the territories opened up by the fur trade led to French government claims of sovereignty over much of North America. However, it was the nature of the fur trade that eventually put an end to such ambitions. This was a business that required the encouragement of Native hunting and trapping over vast areas and, consequently, it required restrictions on agricultural settlement that would have allowed the expansion of the French population. By 1749 North America's French population was still centred in the St. Lawrence Valley, and was outnumbered more than 20 to one by the English colonists along the eastern seaboard. Although the French travelled through and claimed vast territories surrounding the Great Lakes and down the Mississippi to the Gulf of Mexico, English farmers were now expanding westwards across the Appalachian Mountains into the valleys of the Midwest. Within a decade, this situation would come to a head in the battles leading to the English conquest of New France.

In 1749, however, French America was still very much a business empire based on fur. The merchants involved in this profitable trade were among the wealthiest in the colony, and many found it possible to increase their social standing by obtaining a seigneury or even by earning a noble title through appointment to high public office. By 1749 most seigneurs could trace their ancestry to merchant or even habitant origin. Such mobility increased the social complexity of New France, as did the differences in status and custom between people born in France and those born in the colony. Most of the French who came to North America did so on a temporary basis, as appointed officials, soldiers, or tradesmen and servants indentured for a specific period. The majority returned home after their allotted time, while only a few—approximately 10,000 over the 150 years of the colony's existence—stayed on to settle and raise families. As in most colonial societies, there was a clear distinction between the French-born portion of the population and the locally born, with each group considering itself socially, culturally and (according to Kalm) even physically superior to the other. Similar feelings had developed between the inhabitants of Quebec City's administrative capital and Montréal's fur-trade centre. Montréalers were thought to have acquired many of the traits of the Indians with whom they travelled and traded, and were referred to as "Wolves"; in turn, they spoke of the Quebecers as "Sheep." Kalm, whose interest in the women of New France is very apparent, described Montréal women as having a "savage dignity," and considered them to be more attractive and competent than their Quebec City counterparts; Quebec City women, on the other hand, approached those born in France by possessing more "savoir-vivre." Kalm was surprised to find that almost all of the men and women whom he met could read and write, and that class boundaries were not as apparent as in Europe.

Some members of the population had little chance to participate in the social mobility that characterized New France. These were bondservants, who were indentured to their masters for a specific period of time, and slaves. Most of the latter were Indians from the Mississippi Valley who had been captured in warfare by the Indian allies of the French; few of these slaves survived for long when exposed to the diseases circulating among the French population. The remainder of the slaves were Afro-Caribbeans from French colonies in the south; this group stood a greater chance of survival and—perhaps—of gaining freedom for themselves or their children.

Kalm spent a few weeks in and around Quebec City before travelling back upriver to Montréal, and then onwards to New York and Philadelphia. The published account of his travels gives a rare snapshot of a unique society as seen by an outsider who was interested in most aspects of local life. As the only European to visit and write in detail about both the English and French colonies of North America, his comparisons of the two are especially revealing. His portrayal of New France was so glowing, in contrast to his descriptions of New York and Pennsylvania, that the editor of the first English translation of his work added a preface noting that, for political reasons, Kalm was obviously prejudiced against the English. Whether or not his descriptions were politically motivated, Kalm's portrait of habitant life does seem to be overly positive. We might suspect that the hosts accompanying him during most of his visit had no direct experience of the hardships, crop failures and other miseries that were an inevitable part of all early agricultural societies. Or, that if they did know of such problems, and of the sharp dealings and intrigue that were common in the colonial government and the fur trade, then they neglected to mention them to their distinguished visitor.

Kalm was delighted by most of what he saw in New France, and by most of the people whom he encountered. He considered the French of the St. Lawrence Valley to be more prosperous, carefree, polite and better educated than citizens of the English colonies. His portrait of a dynamic and relatively sophisticated society is far from the commonly painted picture of New France as a small, isolated community dominated by priests. To an educated scientist from Northern Europe, the people of New France were fortunate to be part of a society that was—in his view—extraordinarily successful, agreeable and secure. Whether or not Pehr Kalm's descriptions avoided or overlooked the negative aspects of life in New France, a reader of his journal is not surprised that the society he described had the strength and coherence to survive the English conquest that would occur a decade later, and continues to develop in the contemporary world.

August 1755

6. *Acadia*

August 1755

The harvest season arrived with the usual brilliant days of late summer. As in every other year, the massive tides surged up the Baie des Français, the swell dispersing into the red mud channels at the head of the bay. Each year for over a century the dykes built along the tide line had been extended, and the rich fields behind them yielded increased harvests as small farming settlements multiplied along the coast. But this was to be the last summer for a way of life that had been developed by the small group of families on the shores of the Bay of Fundy who called themselves "Acadians."

ENGRAVING OF ACADIAN FARMERS MAKING
HAY BEHIND THE DYKES OF A TIDAL LANDSCAPE.

To the ancient Greeks, the name "Arcadia" referred to a land of pastoral beauty and simple contented people. In 1524, the navigator Giovanni da Verrazzano, exploring westwards for the King of France, gave the name to a pleasant region of America's mid-Atlantic coast. By the following century the name had changed to "Acadie," and the location had shifted northwards to apply to the lands around what is now the Bay of Fundy. French settlement of the region had begun with the fur-trading outpost established in 1605 at Port Royal by Samuel de Champlain and Pierre du Gua de Monts. But fur and codfish were the economic focus of European interest in Canada, and Acadie could not compete with the fur trade of the St. Lawrence Valley or the fishery off the coasts of Cape Breton Island and Newfoundland. When the Port Royal settlement was abandoned in 1607 and Champlain turned his attention to his new and more profitable settlement at Quebec City, French government and commercial interests in the area declined.

Over the following years, however, some of the original settlers returned to Acadie where they were joined by survivors of other unsuccessful settlements, refugees from the hard life of the fishing fleets, nomadic fur traders and, eventually, an occasional missionary. By 1650, a scattering of families had established themselves along the banks of the Rivière Dauphine, near the original Port Royal settlement on what is now Nova Scotia's Annapolis River. The Bay of Fundy tides that flowed up the river had created extensive salt marshes that for millennia had been flooded by high tides with nutrient-rich sea water. By building extensive systems of dykes and draining the marshes behind them, the Acadians created very productive farmland. Most of the Acadian families were from the lowlands of western France, and they imported their ingenious systems of dykes and sluices from their homelands.

These techniques encouraged intensive farming of strips of land along the river, where the soil was fertile and there were no forests to clear. Most of the settlers' food was provided by crops of wheat, oats, rye, peas, flax and vegetables, along with fish and seabirds from the estuary. Small herds of cattle and sheep, together with pigs and poultry, supplied meat, milk, eggs, feathers, wool and leather. The Acadians' small-scale farming of marshlands did not interfere significantly with the traditional way of life of the local Mi'kmaq, whose numbers had been greatly diminished by the introduction of European diseases. A mutually beneficial trade in furs developed between Mi'kmaq and Acadians, supplying a resource that could be exchanged for the metalwork, pottery and other items of European technology that were needed by both peoples.

By successfully adapting a rural European way of life to the New World, the early Acadians seem indeed to have discovered Arcadia. Along the Fundy coast they found freedom from the three major hazards of European life: recurring famine, deadly epidemics and—for young men—forced enrolment in the armies that routinely slaughtered one another throughout the seventeenth and eighteenth centuries. Official attempts to establish a feudal seigneurial system were never successful, and the Acadians evolved their own family-based society. Evidence of their freedom and security is seen in the rate at which the Acadian population grew, despite the fact that there was very little immigration after the early decades. From less than 400 people counted in the first census in 1671, the population increased to about 1,200 in 1701 and over 2,500 in 1715. By the 1750s, the population had grown to over 10,000, and Acadian settlements had expanded to the extensive tidal marshlands at the head of the Bay of Fundy.

What the Acadians had gained in the way of economic security, however, they paid for in political uncertainty. From the time of their first arrival in the area, sovereignty over their lands had been disputed between England and France. Acadia lay between the empire of New France, extending from the St. Lawrence River to the Mississippi River, and the rapidly growing colonies of New England, along the seaboard from Maine to the Carolinas. Neither the government of France nor that of England had much interest in the tide-land farmers who lived along the coast between these regions and who owned little of value to anyone but themselves. Acadia did, however, become a small pawn in the great political games that set England against France and Protestant against Catholic for most of the seventeenth and eighteenth centuries. Time and time again the region changed hands through military conquest, only to be returned under the terms of treaties that occasionally interrupted the war. The Acadians adapted quickly to the situation, declaring themselves neutral and offering little support to either side. While language and religion connected them to France, their economy was increasingly tied to the English colonies at Boston and elsewhere along the Atlantic Coast, where markets existed for their agricultural products. The Acadians' ambiguous position prevented most of their young men from fighting in either

colonial army, while their poverty meant that they escaped the attention of tax collectors and other officers from either of the powers claiming sovereignty over their lands.

But this privileged way of life could not last. By the 1750s, the two powers were closing in on Acadia. France had spent decades building a massive fortress at Louisbourg on Cape Breton Island, in order to protect its fishing fleets and to declare permanent ownership of the region. England had countered with its fortress and naval base at Halifax, and with an increasing number of Scottish, English and Protestant European immigrants settled in various regions of Nova Scotia. The confrontation was repeated on a miniature scale in Acadia, with the French Fort Beauséjour facing the English Fort Lawrence across the marshlands on the isthmus between what are today New Brunswick and Nova Scotia. In July 1755, the English governor of Nova Scotia summoned the leading men from Acadian communities to Halifax, informed them that their commitment to neutrality was no longer adequate, and demanded that they and their people sign an oath of allegiance to England. Some of the leaders signed the oath under protest, but most Acadians insisted on their traditional neutrality. The English governor remained unconvinced that the Acadians could be trusted to remain neutral during the expected conflict over sovereignty of the entire region, and a decision was taken to remove this potential opposition before tackling the French military forces at Louisbourg. In the late summer of 1755, the Acadians were told that they must leave their homes, their farms, their animals and most of their belongings, and that ships would be provided to transport them out of Nova Scotia.

This was a well-planned military operation involving co-ordination with the governors of the New England colonies, who were persuaded to supply ships and accept the displaced population. The process began in September 1755 and, during the following months, over 3,000 Acadians were put aboard ship—some at bayonet-point—and dispersed among the colonies between Massachusetts and Georgia. Their villages were burned to dishearten those who had escaped deportation

CHAMPLAIN'S DRAWING OF THE HABITATION OF PORT ROYAL IN 1607.

by hiding in the woods, and most such refugees fled to French territory in Prince Edward Island, New Brunswick, Quebec or Cape Breton Island. When Louisbourg was captured and destroyed by the English in 1758, another 3,000 Cape Breton Acadians were deported to France. Others were sent to Quebec City when the English occupied Prince Edward Island, only to be dispatched by the French to occupy the tiny islands of St. Pierre and Miquelon off the south coast of Newfoundland. In subsequent years many of the Acadians who had been sent to France or New England, where most lived as impoverished exiles, emigrated once more, this time to Louisiana, where the name "Acadian" was transformed to "Cajun." Others settled in places as distant as the Falkland Islands.

The expulsion of the Acadians is the earliest and best known Canadian example of a type of operation that has become familiar in the contemporary world and which, since the Balkan conflicts of the 1990s, has been given the euphemism "ethnic cleansing." Although this early instance of the process was less bloody than others carried out more recently, it had the same motive: to clear the land of people whose loyalty the governing power did not trust, and it resulted in the same exodus of panic-stricken refugees who had lost not merely their homes and possessions but their entire way of life. It was also similar to the modern instances in that it had only a temporary effect on the ethnic characteristic of the region "cleansed."

Shortly after the war between England and France came to an end in 1763, Acadians who had found life elsewhere to be intolerable began to filter back into their homelands around the Bay of Fundy. Most found their original farms occupied by English-speaking immigrants, and were forced to settle on poorer upland farms. Others moved north along the New Brunswick coast or to the western coast of Cape Breton Island where, over the following decades, they established a way of life based on a seasonal mix of inshore fishing, small-scale farming, woodcutting, boat-building and related trades. Despite official policies suppressing the Catholic religion and the French language, by 1800 the Acadian population had grown close to its numbers at the time of the expulsion and, by the late nineteenth century, it had expanded over ten times more.

It has now been 250 years since the expulsion of the Acadians, years during which the descendants of those who returned have fought for and gradually achieved recognition and acceptance of their language, their religion and their unique culture. Although they now form a significant and well-integrated part of society in Atlantic Canada, the Acadians maintain a form of the neutrality that served them so well in their first centuries of existence: an insistence that they are neither Anglo-Canadians nor French Québecois.

Most Acadians can trace their family names—Arsenault, Boudreau, Gallant, Leblanc and Robichaud, among a few dozen others—to the early settlers of the Fundy tide lands. The dykes built by their ancestors to reclaim farmland along the Rivière Dauphine still stand and now flank the Annapolis Tidal Generating Station, North America's first tidal power plant. If proposals for major electrical generation projects in the Bay of Fundy are realized, Acadians will once again be harnessing the tides around which their ancestors built their lives.

February 1784

7. Loyalists and Yankees

February 1784

The winter had been the mildest that anyone could remember, and for this the governor of the colony was truly thankful. The weather brought little consolation to the thousands of exiles packed into his small city, most of them experiencing their first Nova Scotia winter. To people from Maryland or the Carolinas who had now committed themselves to this northern land, the months of cold rain and wet snow were both miserable and alarming. After seven years of war, the loss of their homes and property, and a confused evacuation from the newly triumphant American republic, Halifax was a dreary and unpromising sanctuary.

A VIEW OF HALIFAX PAINTED IN 1757 SHOWS A
SMALL SETTLEMENT WITH A BUSY HARBOUR.

But most were surviving—the governor and other officers charged with caring for the refugees knew only too well how many would have died had winter brought its usual temperatures, minimally protected as they were by the poorly heated barracks, and huts of boards and canvas that had been hastily constructed the previous autumn.

These refugees of 1784 were experiencing the hardships known to many of Halifax's residents, who had memories of earlier winters spent in similar circumstances. Only 35 years before, Colonel Edward Cornwallis had chosen this magnificent harbour as a bulwark of British power in struggles with the French for control of North America. The British needed a strong military base to counter Louisbourg, the massive French fortress at the eastern tip of Cape Breton Island; although Louisbourg had been captured by the English a few years before, it was now to be returned to the French under treaty. In early July of 1749, Cornwallis's fleet of 13 transports had put 2,500 settlers ashore. Many were discharged war veterans who had been promised farming land, tools and supplies for a year, but more were unemployed and impoverished men and women who had come straight from the streets of London to be dropped into the wilderness with few skills and less will. A regiment of soldiers who had been based at Louisbourg set to work building a small wooden fort atop what is now Citadel Hill, as well as a palisade to protect the community from attack. By the onset of winter the forest inside the palisade had been cleared, streets had been laid out and lined with houses—most of them makeshift huts sheltering people who had already decided to leave the settlement as quickly as possible. Fear of attack by Mi'kmaq

soldiers, who were allied with the French and had killed four workmen across the harbour in September, prevented most from straying outside the palisade. Typhus swept through the town, killing hundreds who were already weakened by the unexpected cold, and poor living conditions. Hundreds more departed on the first available ships.

Making up for the loss of these first settlers, Halifax soon became a magnet for refugees from the fishing industry in Nova Scotia and neighbouring colonies. These were mostly indentured Irishmen, who saw the town as a haven where they could sell their labour and escape virtual slavery. It also attracted merchants and entrepreneurs from the American colonies, who foresaw the immense sums of money that the British would pour into their base for the expected war with the French. Ships from England and Europe brought parties of immigrants selected in accord with Britain's new policy of settling Nova Scotia with Protestants in order to counteract the Catholic Acadian and Mi'kmaq populations. In its first year of existence, Halifax saw the arrival of 1,500 German and Swiss settlers, although they could not be provided with farmland for fear of attacks from the French and Mi'kmaq. Instead, the Europeans were housed for two years in temporary barracks at the edge of town, before being settled at what was to become Lunenburg. Other immigrant groups were maintained in similar camps before being provided with land elsewhere in the colony.

During the 1750s, the city's fortunes were closely tied to the sporadic war with the French: declining when peace held and advancing when the garrison was expanded and the harbour

BY THE LATE 1700s, HALIFAX HAD BEEN TRANSFORMED INTO A MAJOR TOWN.

was filled with ships provisioning for war. When Louisbourg was captured in 1758, demolition crews removed some of the cut stone that faced its buildings—originally taken from old Roman quarries in France—for use in Halifax. By 1760 the streets behind the waterfront boasted two sizeable churches and several other imposing buildings. The end of the war with France also brought a major change in the city's population. The British withdrew a considerable number of their fleet as well as the majority of the soldiers guarding the fort, but their place was taken by a new wave of immigrants from both Europe and New England. With the French military withdrawn from the region after 1760, their Mi'kmaq allies soon concluded treaties with the English and opened the way for settlement throughout a large part of the colony. The most numerous arrivals were New Englanders searching for farmland that was no longer available in their home colonies. Several thousand moved north during the 1760s, taking over much of the land previously farmed by the now-exiled Acadians. In addition, Protestant Irish immigrants arrived from Ulster and, in 1773, the first ship in what was to be a major migration of Highland Scots landed its cargo at Pictou.

Throughout this period Halifax grew slowly, outpaced by several other towns around the coast of Nova Scotia. However, it quickly regained its supremacy in 1776 with the outbreak of the American Revolution and the arrival of another influx of refugees: the families of military men and civil officers evacuated from Boston when that city fell to the republicans. With Boston lost, Halifax inevitably became Britain's most important military base in America. The fortifications on Citadel Hill and elsewhere around the harbour

Encampment of the Loyalists at Johnston, a New Settlement, on the Banks of the River St. Laurence in Canada, taken June taken from A marked in the Plan

ENCAMPMENT OF LOYALISTS ARRIVING AT JOHNSTOWN (NOW CORNWALL) IN EASTERN ONTARIO.

were strengthened. The harbour filled with transports supplying the British armies in America, and with naval ships plundering American vessels or protecting British ships and coastal settlements from American privateers. For the seven years of the war, huge profits could be made in supplying the British military, as well as in more clandestine trading with merchants in Boston and other American ports.

The American Revolution may have begun in 1776 as a rebellion of local governments against accountability to the British Parliament, but it very soon took on the aspect of a civil war. The American leaders' republican aspirations were far from unanimously held by the people of the colonies,

and it is estimated that up to 40 per cent of the population either sympathized with or actively supported the British cause. These included families who held posts in the civil government and the Church of England, men who served in the British military and allied Loyalist units, and many recent immigrants who had assumed that they were coming to live under British rule and had not been caught up in the growing republican feelings of the 1760s and 1770s.

At the end of the war, many of these "Tories" or "Loyalists" found that they were no longer welcome in the American colonies. Those in high office were removed from their positions and had their lands and possessions expropriated. Those who had served with the British military found they had no homes to return to. Even those who had merely sympathized with the British cause faced threats, abuse, even violence and death. Exile was the only answer for such people, and over 80,000 escaped to Britain, to the British islands in the

Caribbean, and to the loyal colonies that would later become parts of Canada. Approximately 20,000 people fled to Nova Scotia (which, at the time, included what is now southern New Brunswick), doubling the colony's population within a single year. The British government had promised pensions for disbanded military men and the holders of civil offices, as well as compensation for property expropriated and provisions for the first year in their place of exile. Loyalists who hoped to continue farming dispersed to Annapolis, the Saint John River Valley, the new town of Shelburne, and other localities. Halifax received some hopeful farmers, but took in a larger number of those more accustomed to urban life, ranging from holders of high office in New York or Charleston, to tradesmen, to waterfront vagrants attracted by the promise of a year's support.

The first Loyalist immigrant fleets began arriving at Nova Scotia ports in April, having sailed from New York, which was held by the British throughout most of 1783 and where exiles from a large part of the Atlantic Coast had congregated. In preparation, the Nova Scotia government had expropriated over half a million hectares of land that had been granted earlier but never taken up, and stockpiled food and construction materials. Some of the early arrivals were able to select farmland that summer, and received enough timber and shingles to build small houses. However, the Loyalists who disembarked from ships during the later summer months found less available land and fewer supplies. The largest fleets began to arrive in September and continued into November, when New York was turned over to the Americans. These refugees found themselves facing the northern winter with no homes and

scant resources. Halifax more than doubled its population with the arrival of these immigrants, who took any room available in existing houses, crowded into hurriedly built and inadequately heated shelters, filled the churches, and lived aboard ships in the harbour. A military regiment spent the winter in huts and tents erected in the forest outside the town.

Tradition has created a picture of the Loyalist ancestors of so many Canadians as the very British upper crust of American society: honest landowners and men of affairs who were willing to discard all of their possessions for loyalty to the British cause. Halifax did receive its share of such families, but they were a small proportion of the flood of immigrants who arrived in 1783. More common were the soldiers of disbanded regiments and German mercenary units, along with ordinary farmers and workmen, many of whom were recent immigrants from the British Isles and Europe. About one in ten of the Loyalists who arrived were Black: either slaves accompanying their owners or freedmen who had served the British cause. Over the coming years, Halifax would attract many more Black families who had originally landed elsewhere in Nova Scotia hoping to obtain farmland, but had been passed over by local authorities in favour of white immigrants. Many of the arrivals on the later ships were Loyalist only in name, a mix of drifters and entrepreneurs who, predicting Halifax's future as the major trading port between Britain and the West Indies, had a purely monetary interest in the city.

Although the winter of 1783–1784 was mild by local standards, many of the recent arrivals were dismayed by both the weather and the apparent lack of opportunity in their new homeland. Their outlook was not improved by poor living conditions, overcrowding and the high prices charged for food and accommodation. Neither were they appreciative of their hosts, whom they accused of profiting from their misery. The inner circle of families that controlled most of the city's businesses were viewed—with some justification—as Yankee sympathizers who had made money by dealing with both sides in the recent conflict. Halifax was certainly not a happy city in 1784, when the officer responsible for providing supplies to the immigrants wrote of "all the idle vagrants who had been loitering about the streets of the metropolis & were daily committing irregularities." In December of the same year, a London newspaper reported that "Disbanded Soldiers are Daily and Nightly picked up in the Streets in a perishing state & sent to the poor House afflicted with various Disorders."

The city's population soon began to decline as exiles moved elsewhere in the colony to take up farmland, and others abandoned Nova Scotia for more profitable destinations. In the following years, Halifax gradually became less of a refugee camp, taking on the character of a provincial capital that had suddenly doubled in size through an influx of citizens from the American colonies. The military presence returned in force as the American Revolution threatened to re-emerge as the War of 1812, and British officers and civil officials formed an elite that vied for local power and prestige with the body of Yankee merchants and entrepreneurs that had emerged from the population of Loyalists and earlier settlers. The city was fed by Loyalist farms along the adjacent valleys, and by an inshore fishing industry that soon occupied every cove of the Nova Scotia shore. The vessels constructed by shipbuilders of

Halifax and other Nova Scotia towns began to gain renown in the maritime world, and sailors enlivened the downtown streets as Halifax became the heart of the shipping trade between Britain and America, and the centre of the West Indies trade of salt fish in exchange for fruit and rum. The miseries of 1783 and 1784 would be remembered as part of a painful but temporary episode that was vital to the development of a unique and exciting city.

June 1835

8. The Shiners' War

June 1835

The month of June invariably brings the first summer days of subtropical heat to the Ottawa Valley, yet the intensity of the heat never fails to surprise us. So it was in the summer of 1835: the air was still and humid beneath a pitiless sun, and the men steering immense rafts of squared timber dipped their caps in the cold river to find relief. They were on their way from the logging camps of the upper Ottawa River to the wharfs at Quebec City, where the rafts would be dismantled and the timber loaded aboard ships for Britain. Bytown was the first stop on their long journey, and most of the crews chose to pause there, despite the newly built timber slide that allowed them to bypass the churning cauldron of the Chaudière Falls and avoid the need to either dismantle the raft or risk a hazardous run through the rapids.

Coming ashore to drink, and to sleep in real beds for the first time in months, the raftsmen found their own allotted section in the Bytown settlement that had already divided itself into distinct communities. The centre was Barracks Hill—where Canada's Parliament Buildings now stand—with its military quarters and hospital built a decade before, during the construction of the Rideau Canal. Upper Town sloped away to the south and west, a few streets of brick and stone houses occupied by the English and Scottish gentry of the settlement, merging into farmland originally cleared to feed the men and horses who built the canal. Across the canal to the east lay Lower Town, a jumble of muddy streets, log buildings and shacks built from boards and turf. Lower Town was home to the Irish labourers who had immigrated to work on the canal, the families of French Canadians who provided most of the labour in the logging camps, and the hotels, taverns and brothels that catered to the raftsmen. Upstream, where the Chaudière Falls tumbled through a clump of limestone islands, came the industrial sounds of whining water-powered sawmills and thumping machinery, mingled with the shouts of teamsters and the occasional heavy splash as a raft plunged from the timber slide.

On a hot day the town looked sleepy and peaceful, but in the early summer of 1835 a heavy uneasiness hung over both the stylish salons of Upper Town and the raucous taverns below Rideau Street. Both sides of the town drew their lifeblood from the logging industry. The large houses of Upper Town were occupied by the men who owned the timber rights and logging camps of the upper Ottawa Valley, the Chaudière sawmills, and the warehouses that supplied food

and equipment to the camps. The farmers in the surrounding countryside, mostly retired British military men or immigrants from Scotland and Protestant Ireland, depended on the camps as a market for their wheat, oats, beans, pork and hay. Most of the French-speaking inhabitants of Lower Town made their living as loggers and teamsters in the camps, and as raftsmen on the voyages to Quebec City. Since the town had grown up around the cutting and transport of timber, the citizens had learned to tolerate the arrival of the raftsmen each spring, and the general disorder they caused on their way downriver. This spring the trouble had been more widespread and violent than usual—and even worse was expected. Bytown in 1835 housed a mix of ethnic and social tensions that was beyond the control of the few magistrates appointed by the government to maintain order. This was the summer of the Shiners' War.

The logging industry on the Ottawa had begun a generation earlier, with the arrival of Loyalist settlers who found timber more profitable than farming. The Ottawa and its tributaries were surrounded by pine forests with immense trees the size of those that we now associate with the rainforests of the Pacific Coast. Philemon Wright, who founded the industry, had difficulty selling the first raft of such timber that he floated to Quebec City in 1806. However, the market quickly changed two years later when Napoleon Bonaparte organized a trade embargo that cut off Britain's traditional sources of timber from Russia and Scandinavia. The market for Ottawa Valley timber continued to grow even after the embargo collapsed, for Britain was running out of wood. The population was growing rapidly, industry was advancing, and local forests

PAINTING OF A TIMBER RAFT ON THE VOYAGE FROM THE UPPER OTTAWA RIVER TO QUEBEC CITY.

could no longer supply materials for the construction of mills and houses, bridges and canal locks, pit props for mines and, especially, for the hulls and spars of the merchant and naval fleets on which Britain's security and prosperity depended. By 1820, the Ottawa Valley was a major supplier to British shipyards and construction projects.

Logging on the Ottawa was a wasteful business. Only the tallest and straightest trees were felled, only the clearest and soundest logs were cut from the trunks, and much of the wood was chopped away to form a square timber 50 to 80 centimetres across. Areas were soon "logged out" or burnt over by fires igniting in the dry tangle of chips and branches left by the loggers. The lumber frontier moved rapidly upriver beyond the Chaudière, fanning out along the tributary rivers of the upper Ottawa Valley. The work was now carried out from isolated camps established each autumn close to the area to be cut. The first of the men arrived by canoe in late summer, and through the autumn they cut hay from the beaver meadows, built log stables for the horses and oxen, and put up housing for the ten or 20 men in the crew. This "shanty" was a square of walls built from logs, covered by a low roof of poles and bark with a large central opening to provide light and to allow smoke to escape. Beneath this opening was the cooking fire, built on sand in a box of logs, and provided with hooks for hanging kettles and for drying wet clothes. The men sat and slept on benches built against the outer walls, where they were above the icy chill of the dirt floor but still cold enough in a large room heated only by an open fire.

The main crew arrived after freeze-up, by snowshoe or by sled, with the teamsters whose horses and oxen provided the camps' motive power. With the onset of winter, life was reduced to a very basic routine. The cook wakened the men in the dark and, in most camps, the day began with a shot of rum or local whisky followed by breakfast of bread or hardtack biscuit, salt meat or fish, and potatoes. By the first light of dawn, the animals had been fed and harnessed, and the crew were following the camp foreman down the snowy skid road to the next stand of trees to be felled. A team of axemen felled each tree and then chopped off the upper part of the trunk, from the first branches to the tip. Another crew of axemen removed the outer portions of the log, leaving a square piece of timber that the teamsters then hauled to the river's edge. Work continued until dark, broken only by a noon meal that was identical to breakfast but often included pea soup. When it was too dark and too cold to carry on, the foreman called the day and the crew trailed

THE ENTRANCE TO THE RIDEAU CANAL PAINTED IN 1839, WITH TIMBER RAFTS IN THE FOREGROUND AND BARRACKS HILL (NOW PARLIAMENT HILL) TO THE RIGHT.

back to the shanty for another meal of salt pork and beans, potatoes, bread and molasses, and scalding tea. By the light of a cooking fire, the men sharpened their axes, smoked, drank what whisky was available, and soon rolled into their blankets as the intense cold of the icy night crept through the log walls. The winter's work ended only with spring breakup, when the men rafted the logs together and floated them downstream, dropping off the crew at Bytown and Montréal, keeping only those needed to steer the giant raft to Quebec City and the biggest party of the year.

In the early years of the industry, most of the crews were homesteaders who were selling the trees cut from their own lots, or were logging during the winter while their wives worked the family farm as well as caring for the children. By the 1830s, about 3,000 men were working in the camps, and most of these were professional loggers who spent their summers in towns along the rafting routes or on the farms owned by their fathers or older brothers. Most were French Canadians, originally from the farms of the St. Lawrence Valley, who had established a reputation for skill with an axe, hard work, and causing little trouble either in camp or on the rafts. These were important attributes, and so even though the French loggers demanded the highest wages, most of the camp owners and foremen hired as many as they could. But in 1832, with the completion of the Rideau Canal linking Bytown to Lake Ontario, a large body of unemployed labourers began looking for work in the logging industry.

Most of the canal labourers were Irish, imported specifically for this work from the impoverished Catholic counties of central Ireland. For six years they had dug through the muck of an endless swamp, shivering from malaria in the sweltering mosquito-plagued summers and freezing through the endless winters. Hundreds had died and were buried without markers, and most of those who survived finished the task as poverty-stricken as they had begun. With the canal completed, many of these survivors had come to Bytown to look for work, and were huddled in shacks and turf huts along the Lower Town side of the canal. Lacking better facilities, the Irish community used the canal for drinking water and as a sewer. As a result, when cholera reached Bytown in the summer of 1832 and again in 1834, it bypassed the Upper Town but swept through Lower Town, claiming many victims.

The Protestant British of Upper Town had arrived in Canada with fixed views of Irish peasants as violent and untrustworthy animals, and the hungry families living in squalor and disease beside the canal gave them little cause to change their opinions. The Irish needed work to survive, but few citizens of Bytown wanted to hire them. From poverty and hunger, misery and frustration, came desperate determination. If they lacked both the skill and the reputation to obtain work, they could at least put to use the violence that had bought them some respect among the Rideau Canal's labour gangs. Those who did find work in the logging camps were valued by owners who were carving out their own territories by attacking and intimidating crews that had legitimate rights to the trees.

Violent encounters were common in the logging camps, as were fights between French and Irish rafting crews on the river. By 1835, the Irish had found a leader, an adventurer named Peter Aylen who had jumped ship in Canada, made good and now owned his own logging camps. Under his guidance, the unemployed labourers set out to take over the jobs held by the French. In the spring of that year, several rafts with French crews were attacked, the men thrown off and the rafts broken up or hijacked. The French fought back, and one of their foremen named Jos Montferrand became a heroic figure in Ottawa Valley legend, known to the French under his own name and to the English as "Joe Mufferaw."

Many of the Irish rafting crews stayed in Bytown rather than continuing the voyage to Quebec City—rafts with Irish crews were being hijacked as they passed Montréal—and began to organize themselves under the name of "Shiners." Lower Town became a perilous place for those who were not Irish, as hundreds of Shiners caroused in the taverns and wandered the streets, beating up Frenchmen, insulting women, and taunting any gentry who passed by. A few citizens were murdered, a French-owned tavern was burned, and Shiners took over the bridges across the Chaudière islands, where they opened a bar, collected tolls, and threw opponents into the roiling river. By June, Bytown's one effective magistrate found himself in the position of many small-town sheriffs in Hollywood westerns. He resigned his appointment on the grounds that citizens were so intimidated they would neither support him as deputies nor make the necessary convictions as jurors. At this stage, the Shiners could have taken control of Bytown, but they contented themselves with random beatings and general troublemaking. In one mischievous move, tellingly aimed at the town's British upper classes, they packed the annual business meeting of the local Agricultural Society,

voted out the gentry farmers and hobby gardeners, and installed Shiners as officers of the society.

Violence continued throughout the summer of 1835 but, in late October when many of the loggers were leaving for the camps upriver, the citizens of Bytown—in western-movie tradition—formed a vigilante committee to clean up the stragglers. The Shiners' War was over and a growing number of camp owners now saw advantages in hiring Irish workers, both for the low wages that they would accept and as insurance against the Irish employees of competing crews. Sporadic trouble continued in the camps and along the rafting route for several years, and for the rest of the century the logging woods of the upper Ottawa Valley were segregated into French and Irish camps as the sons and grandsons of Canal labourers became an essential force in the lumber trade. Ethnic violence gradually subsided as men worked together, as women became neighbours, and as Catholic families intermarried to create the unique culture and society of the upper Ottawa Valley. By the twentieth century, the hostility was preserved only in the schoolyard, where the violence of the past remained as a ritual hatred that is well remembered by many people living in Ottawa today.

July 1840

9. The Métis of Red River

July 1840

Summer on the northern Plains was always a time of plenty. The grass grew tall and succulent in the moist heat of cloudless days, and the buffalo began to accumulate thick layers of fat to see them through the coming winter. Spring calves usually survived the summer to increase the herds, and as the animals moved in search of fresh pasture they formed vast throngs that covered the countryside. Wolves and grizzly bears worked the fringes of the herds, while flocks of crows and magpies patrolled the wake of the moving sea of animals. For thousands of years, the Indigenous peoples of the area took few buffalo during this season, allowing the animals to fatten on summer grazing and the mothers to raise and protect their calves. Their major buffalo hunts took place in the autumn, when the animals were in prime condition.

MÉTIS CAMP ON THE PRAIRIE.

Hunters drove the herds into log-built pounds or over the low cliffs and abrupt ravines of the Plains landscape, dried the meat for winter use and took the thick hides for clothing and tipi covers. With the coming of horses and guns, hunters could ride directly into a herd and kill from the saddle, a dangerous but efficient means of obtaining meat and hides.

By the early 1800s, a new hunting pattern had emerged on the eastern Plains: a massive industrial slaughter that was carried out in the summer so that meat could be dried and transported to the northern fur-trade posts before the onset of winter. These hunts were undertaken by the growing population of Métis who had moved into the grasslands from the fur-trading posts and canoe routes of the northern forest. The Métis population and its unique way of life emerged as a result of frequent marriages between European fur traders and the Native women among whose families they lived. The children of these marriages usually found employment in the fur trade, some paddling the great freight canoes that carried the furs to Montréal or Hudson Bay; others as clerks or traders and, occasionally, as governors of substantial trading posts. As generations passed, the Métis developed an identity and culture of their own, one that flourished and spread with the constant travel along the corridors of the northwestern fur trade. The Métis were not an isolated or backward people in any sense. Almost all were fluently bilingual in French and Cree, the primary languages of the fur trade; most could converse in Anishinabe or Assiniboine or another Indigenous language, or in the Gaelic and English spoken by the Scots and English employed by the Hudson's Bay Company and by their Métis descendants. Spending their lives in trading communities that saw a continual flow of travellers bringing news from London and Montréal, the Métis were familiar not only with the latest technology but also with the political developments in distant Canada, the United States and Europe.

In the 1820s, the fur trade was reorganized as the beaver of the northern forests became "trapped out"; many posts were closed and their Métis employees put out of work. However, the remaining fur traders still needed to be fed, and the food that fuelled the commerce of the northwestern posts and canoe routes was pemmican: dried buffalo meat mixed with berries and rendered buffalo fat. Many Métis joined relatives who had earlier moved onto the eastern Plains to take part in the lucrative hunt that supplied this necessity. Small Métis settlements appeared along the Saskatchewan and Assiniboine River Valleys, but by far the largest hunt was organized from the villages and small farms clustered around the junction of the Assiniboine and Red Rivers, where Winnipeg stands today but which was then known as the Red River settlement.

The settlement found itself at the intersection of the most important travel routes in the eastern Plains: the canoe brigades from Montréal and the Great Lakes passed through the southern end of Lake Winnipeg, only a few kilometres downstream; the overland route to the Saskatchewan River and the far northwest followed the Assiniboine Valley; and the Red River provided the most direct access to the growing commercial centres of the Mississippi Valley. In 1811, the lower Red River had been chosen by Lord Selkirk as a site for establishing a colony of Scottish farmers and, although many of the original settlers soon dispersed, the region remained the agricultural and

MÉTIS BUFFALO HUNT ON THE EASTERN PLAINS DURING THE 1840S.

business centre of the fur trade in the northwest. A substantial portion of its commerce was related to the great buffalo hunt organized each summer by the hundreds of Métis families who made up the majority of the population in the region.

Alexander Ross, a retired fur trader, wrote a fascinating and detailed account of the buffalo hunt that he accompanied in 1840. In mid-June, the hunting party assembled about 100 kilometres to the south of the settlement, where the Red River crosses what is now the border that separates Canada and the United States. A roll call produced 1,630 names; about 600 of these were hunters and the remainder were their wives and children, whose duties included drying and processing the meat and driving the high-wheeled Red River carts that transported the hunt's produce. More than 1,200 carts were counted, half of them drawn by horses and the rest by oxen; 400 hunting horses and over 500 dogs also accompanied the party. Ten "captains" were elected, one of whom was named as the leader of the camp and the hunt. Since the party was travelling into the territory of the Lakota, who had previously shown themselves willing and capable of dealing with trespassers, the enterprise was organized in a military fashion, complete with scouts and soldiers, as well as precise instructions on how to form a defensive encampment in case of attack.

For ten days, the expedition trekked slowly southwestwards through oceans of high grass. The line of carts stretched to almost 10 kilometres, and the screeching of their ungreased axles could be heard for a greater distance. In early July, they approached the higher country to the north of the Missouri

River, in what is now North Dakota, and met the buffalo for the first time. The hunt was organized with precision in order to make the best use of surprise and a concerted attack on the herds; on the first day over 1,300 buffalo were killed, and a second hunt a few days later yielded 1,200 animals. In the subsequent weeks, several large hunts and numerous smaller skirmishes probably resulted in more than 10,000 buffalo killed, from which Ross estimated that over 500 tons of pemmican and dried meat were transported back to Red River. The entire hunt lasted over two months and travelled as far as the Missouri River, a round trip of over 500 kilometres.

The 1840 hunt may have been the largest that the Red River Métis ever undertook. Commercial hunts such as these were decimating the buffalo herds of the eastern Plains. In 1851, a slightly smaller Métis hunting party fought a pitched battle with the Lakota, whose lands in what is now South Dakota no longer supported enough animals to satisfy the needs of both groups. In the following decade, the United States Cavalry began to restrict Métis access to the region, seeing them as a possible threat in the developing war that was to rage across the American Plains during the 1860s and 1870s. The hunt gradually shifted from the Red River to the small Métis settlements along the Saskatchewan River, where buffalo could still be found into the 1870s. The Métis who chose to stay near the Red River settlement made their living through a mix of hunting, transporting and trading, while they farmed the narrow lots that their ancestors had laid out along the lower Red River Valley.

The threatened disruption of this way of life, through the expansion of Canadian and American populations and growing political interest in the region, gave rise to the Red River Rebellion of the 1870s. The skills and martial strategies developed during decades of buffalo hunting served the Métis well during this confrontation with the new Dominion of Canada. Fifteen years later this small society made its last military stand in the Saskatchewan River Valley, but by this time the buffalo were almost extinct, and the Métis way of life was threatened by the first major influx of farmers who would transform the Plains from an endless grassland to a checkerboard of cultivated fields. These newcomers even found a use for the bones of buffalo killed during the hunts of earlier times, collecting and exporting them on the newly built railways, to be processed into fertilizer.

The traces left by the Métis society that developed around the buffalo hunt were not as easily extinguished. The founding of Manitoba was largely a Métis accomplishment, as were the efforts—over more than a century—to preserve the rights, language and religion of their buffalo-hunting ancestors. The landmarks left by their society are clearly visible in the French-language schools scattered across the northern Plains. They can even be seen by a traveller flying across this part of the continent: downstream from Winnipeg, the Red River Valley is divided into an array of long and narrow fields fronting on the river, in an arrangement so different from the huge rectangles that make up the surrounding wheat fields, and so reminiscent of the St. Lawrence Valley in the distant province of Quebec. This system of land division, which gave each farmer access to the transportation route provided by the river, as well as close neighbours who formed a continuous village along the riverbanks, remains a tangible mark of the society created by the Red River Métis.

July 12, 1885

10. *A City on a Hill*

July 12, 1885

This was the day that the men of the community walked, following the booming drums and wailing pipes, between fields showing the first yellow tints of ripening grain. Their determined faces perspired in the heat as they crossed the new stone bridge and climbed the hill towards the cluster of church spires at the town's summit. Women and children lined the shady sidewalks to join in the excitement of the parade: the wild blasts of music, the brilliant banners pledging allegiance to the Sovereign and to the God of the Bible, the marching lines of white shirts under bright orange and purple sashes and, finally, King William of Orange on his prancing white horse.

The Loyal Orange Order had been formed 90 years before in Ireland, as a Protestant protective association fighting vehemently against the Catholic religion and the anti-British sentiments of the Irish majority. The Order soon spread to the New World, where it found a natural home among the Protestant Irish, Scots and people of English ancestry who made up the majority of settlers in the Maritimes and Upper Canada. In Canada, the Order's militant anti-Catholicism combined easily with anti-French and anti-Irish sentiments. During the first half of the nineteenth century, the police and even the military were called out repeatedly to quell rioting "Orangemen," or to prevent armed conflict between Orangemen and groups of Catholic French or Irish. The threat was greatest on July 12—the "Glorious Twelfth"—when Orangemen marched to commemorate the Protestant King William of Orange's 1690 defeat of the Catholic King James at the Battle of the Boyne in Ireland.

In most regions of rural Ontario, the population was so overwhelmingly Protestant that by the later nineteenth century it was hard to justify maintaining a militant vigilance against the Catholic threat. In these areas, and in times when cheap whisky flowed less freely on public occasions than it had during the early nineteenth century, the Orange Order gradually took on the nature of a service organization providing support to its members, helping new Protestant immigrants to settle, and raising funds for needy causes. Its membership was so large that the Order had considerable political power, and its support for its own people helped to elect many Orangemen—including Canada's first prime minister—to high political office.

In this less militant environment, Orangemen liked to present themselves as honest citizens rather than as religious bigots, but in July 1885 the anger of the Orangemen was riding high. Throughout the past months, the newspapers had been ablaze with news of another rebellion of the Catholic French-speaking Métis in the West, like the uprising that had been put down at Red River 15 years before. In March, many Ontario towns had waved goodbye to young men joining militia units, travelling west along the route of the almost-completed Canadian Pacific Railway, and then marching north through the mud of a prairie spring towards the guerrilla army awaiting them in the Métis country around the forks of the Saskatchewan River. In late April, the first news of open warfare had trickled down the telegraph lines, followed by reports of casualties among the militia and speculation about an all-out "Indian War" in the northwest. A month later it was all over, and the leader and self-proclaimed prophet Louis Riel was in jail awaiting his trial. On July 6, only six days before the Glorious Twelfth, he had been formally accused of high treason.

If they had bothered to find out, most of the Orange marchers would probably have supported the Métis rebels' demands: clear title to lands that their people had occupied for generations, a representative government, and better treatment of Indians by the Government of Canada. Few Orangemen knew that the rebels were opposed by their priests and had no support from the Catholic Church. But the Métis's simple act of taking up arms against the Sovereign, together with their leader's puzzling declarations of his religious mission, condemned them all in the eyes of the Orangemen. They would use the influence they held at all levels of Canadian society to make certain that Riel's trial could end in nothing but a guilty verdict and an execution. French Canada, fearing that intolerance would make a mockery of the trial, belatedly threw their support behind Riel and the Métis cause. The Dominion of Canada, just 18 years old, faced a summer of rising ethnic and religious tensions.

The ferocity of religious feeling that existed in Victorian Ontario is difficult to comprehend from today's perspective. Suspicion and hatred between Protestants and Catholics was a remnant of the religious wars that had divided Europe since the sixteenth century but, by the mid-nineteenth century this mutual fear and loathing had subsided in most countries. Its survival in Ontario was rooted in the lands from which most immigrants had arrived: the British Isles and, in particular, Ireland. The conflicts that survive in parts of Ulster today provide a sense of the religion-fuelled emotions that prevailed in nineteenth-century Ontario.

Religion not only dominated political opinion during the 1880s but also permeated most aspects of life to a greater extent than at any time in the country's history. The previous century had brought enormous changes in Ontario's populations and way of life. Loyalist refugees, arriving from the new American republic during the 1780s, had cut the first small clearings from the forests along the northern shores of Lakes Ontario and Erie. Throughout the first half of the nineteenth century, agricultural settlement had gradually expanded northwards into the forest, as waves of settlers arrived from the British Isles and elsewhere in Europe. While a few small towns along the Great Lakes, including the capital at York, provided a comfortable existence and something approaching a replica of British society, the vast majority of settlers faced lives of isolation, and the endless work of clearing lots and creating self-sufficient farms.

The poor and often impassable roads linking communities quickly degenerated into bush trails as one moved away from the Great Lakes. Along these roads, a traveller was lucky to encounter a log hotel offering shelter, food and whisky. Where the road dipped to cross a creek, there was the occasional mill supplying local farmers with sawn boards or grinding their grain into flour. Much of the commerce in this backcountry was provided by itinerant peddlers, although some had established small stores in order to sell the few necessities that could not be produced by the farms. The major social occasions were "bees," where neighbours pooled their labour to build a house or barn, cut a clearing for a new settler, or improve a road. These events were fuelled by whisky, which was generously provided in return for free labour, and it's hardly surprising that many settlers considered a bee more trouble than it was worth. Locally distilled whisky was so widely available and so cheap to purchase that its consumption accompanied, and often interfered with, many aspects of Ontario life. The society and culture of the early 1800s were shaped by the competing influences of the gentility of the town's elite and the harsh reality faced by the inhabitants of the clearings.

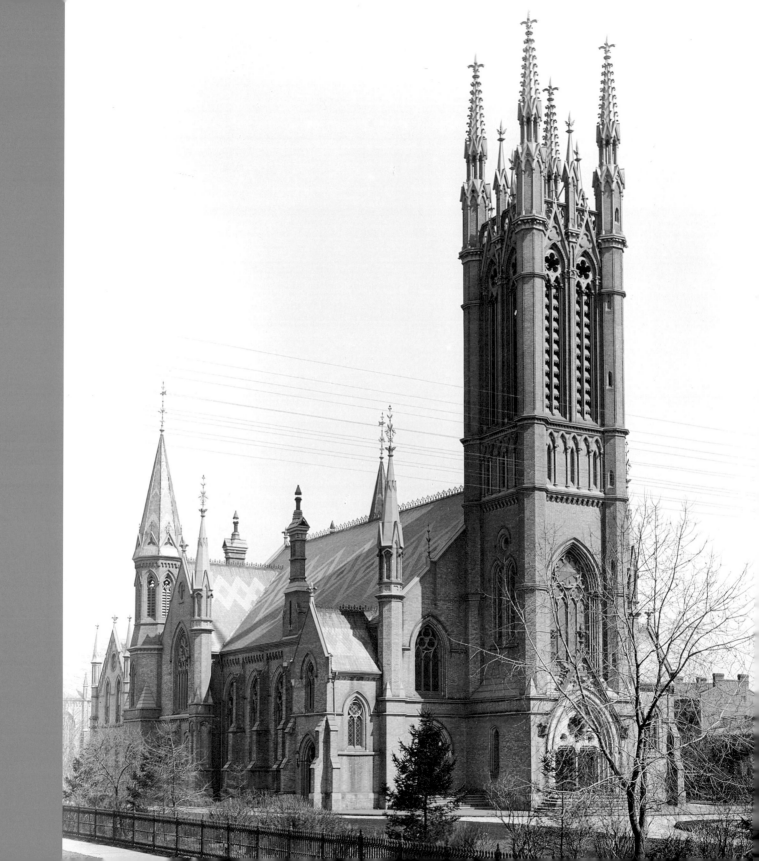

Religion was not a dominant force in this new society. While the Anglican Church was favoured by the upper classes, most early settlers belonged to a variety of Protestant denominations including Presbyterian, Baptist, Congregationist and Methodist. Churches only existed in the established towns and were too distant for the majority of country people to

visit more than occasionally. The rural population was most frequently served by circuit riders: Methodist ministers who held services in houses, barns or in the open fields. The neighbouring families who attended these services supplied food and shelter for the travelling preacher and his horse. For most rural people, the major religious events were summer camp meetings, where a number of preachers joined forces over a few days to revive faith among people who had gathered together from an entire region. These meetings were as much social as religious events, and they tended to be so disorderly that stockades were often built around the meeting ground to keep out whisky-drinking rowdies whose souls had

TWO ORANGE PARADES IN EARLY TWENTIETH-CENTURY ONTARIO: ONE IN A RURAL TOWN AND THE OTHER ON TORONTO'S QUEEN STREET.

not yet been saved. While most people in early nineteenth-century Ontario were Christian believers, few made an outward show of their faith.

By the latter half of the 1800s, conditions had changed re-markably. Through most of what is now southern Ontario, the unrelenting work of clearing fields had been com-pleted and farms were becoming increasingly prosperous. A growing web of steamship and railway lines spanned the province, carrying farm crops for export and providing the transportation needed by a variety of local industries. Waterfalls on the rivers of eastern Ontario now powered spin-ning and weaving mills, while those to the west of Toronto ran machines producing farm equipment, furniture and many other items. The fields around Oil Springs and Petrolia saw the first commercial oil wells in North America, supplying the entire country with kerosene to light its homes and oil to lubricate the machines of Canada's industrial revolution. Brickyards produced the cladding material for most of the farmhouses that were built during the late nineteenth century and which are still occupied today across rural Ontario. The wealth flowing into the province—from sales of grain and other farm produce, wood items and manufactured goods—promoted the rapid growth of towns at lake ports, railroad junctions and sources of water power. By the 1880s, rural Ontario would have been clearly recognizable to a visitor from our day.

However, the beliefs and motives that influenced the work-ings of society would have been less familiar. For example, although public education was a major achievement of the period, it was not embraced as a means of producing an efficient and productive labour force, as it would be today. Instead, Ontario's educational system, established in 1871, was the culmination of a quarter century of effort by Egerton Ryerson, whose Methodist beliefs saw Christian duty as in-cluding the moral and physical improvement of the lives of one's fellow citizens, leading eventually to the perfec-tion of society on Earth. The red-brick schools designed by Ryerson, which are still very familiar to the older generation of Ontarians today, serve as a testament to the optimistic reli-gious beliefs that permeated the society of Victorian Ontario.

The years between 1870 and 1900 also saw a boom in church construction. Congregations that had previously been con-tent with small log or wood-frame buildings in rural villages now had the numbers and the wealth to erect great structures of stone and brick. Revivals of Gothic and Romanesque architecture inspired most churches of the period, and soaring spires and vaulted roofs competed with one another for the attention of both worshippers and passersby. These impos-ing symbols of a community's faith marked a period when religion was emerging as a very public aspect of life for both the individual and the community. It was a time when many citizens of Ontario considered themselves to have been partic-ularly blessed. This feeling can be traced in part to the Loyalist founders of Upper Canada, whose allegiance to the British Crown did not prevent them from bringing with them the American assumption that God had chosen this continent for the establishment of His kingdom. The sentiment was prob-ably reinforced by the fact that Upper Canada was founded later and developed more slowly than the northeastern United

States, so that itinerant ministers and preachers at camp meetings often compared the virtues of this simple frontier society to what they described as the decadent wealth and iniquity of the cities to the south of the Great Lakes.

Ontario's strong attachment to Britain, rooted in the British heritage of most of Upper Canada's citizens and reinforced by successful resistance to American invasion in the War of 1812, also came to acquire religious overtones. As the British Empire expanded around the globe, it assumed its own divinely appointed role as the carrier of Christianity and civilization to humankind. The increase in Protestant missionary outreach in Victorian times was an effort to save the souls of benighted heathens, and also to lead the backward peoples of the world along the path to civilization. The towns and farms of Ontario provided strong support for both these goals of missionary work and, by the 1890s, Toronto was one of the foremost centres of missionary activity in Christendom. The sanctity of the Sunday Sabbath as a day of worship and reflection was more strongly supported in Ontario than in most other Christian nations. The temperance movement also found many champions in a society that could well remember the alcoholic excesses of the past.

As a society that was overwhelmingly British, Protestant and proudly more virtuous than the free and dissolute societies of the Old World and the United States, Ontario liked to portray itself as a "City on a Hill" and a light to the world (*Matthew 5:14* "You are the light of the world. A city set on a hill cannot be hid."). The biblical metaphor was made apparent in the architecture of towns built at this time, in which the most prominent elevation provided a setting for an array of churches. Their cluster of spires afforded travellers their first glimpse of the town, and was a constant reminder to the townspeople of their faith and the blessings that arose from it. For a few decades, the people of Ontario could sustain the conviction that their society had been divinely chosen to serve as an inspiration to the world. But it was a belief that could not survive the horrors of twentieth-century war, the rapid growth of urban society, and the throngs of immigrants with different religions and community memories, whose mere presence brought knowledge and recognition of a wider world.

The fate of the Orange Order is a good measure of the declining power of belief in Ontario's righteousness. By the early twentieth century, the Order had lost much of its capacity to elect public officials and to terrorize Catholic neighbours. The July 12 parades began to fade in the years after the First World War, and dwindled again when soldiers returned from a Europe ravaged by the Second World War. Small marches could still be found in a shrinking number of rural areas until the 1960s, but that decade of social protest and cultural turmoil stamped out the last embers of the Order as a public force and, with it, the belief in Ontario as a City on a Hill.

January 7, 1908

11. *Settling the Prairies*

January 7, 1908

The church was a small shell of warmth and light, surrounded by the frozen silence of the winter night. The aromas of newly sawn wood, fresh paint and kerosene mingled with the pungent incense of this first Christmas Eve service in the new church. A few hours earlier most of the people assembled here had eaten the Holy Supper in small log houses and sod-roofed dugouts scattered in clearings recently cut from the surrounding bush. Some had walked to church in felt boots, their path lit only by the setting crescent moon. Those with teams of horses had bumped along snowy bush trails in farm box sleds packed with straw, gathering neighbours along the way. Now, shoulder to shoulder, they filled the church with the warmth of human bodies and the glow of human spirits.

AN ESTABLISHED FARM LIKE THIS ONE, BUILT BY UKRAINIAN IMMIGRANTS ON THE NORTHERN PRAIRIES DURING THE EARLY TWENTIETH CENTURY, WAS THE RESULT OF MANY YEARS OF HARDSHIP AND LABOUR.

The familiar movements of the priest, the deep-voiced recitation of the litany followed by the small choir's responses, and the glow of icons in the lamplight brought to mind Christmas masses last attended in the village churches of Galicia and Bukovina. And with them came memories of the intervening years—years that had brought great changes in the lives of all those crowded into the little building.

The 1880s and 1890s saw a gradually swelling stream of immigrant farmers who were drawn to Canada by the promise of free land in the West. The Canadian Pacific Railway was completed in 1885, and early farmers had proved that wheat could flourish in the deep black soils of the grasslands stretching from the forests of Ontario to the Rocky Mountains. By this time, the buffalo were almost extinct, and with them had gone the hunting culture of the Plains Indians whose land this had once been. The Canadian government had good reasons for wanting to fill these vast landscapes with a farming population: the wheat and other cereal crops that they produced would increase Canada's exports, the farmers would provide a market for goods manufactured in Eastern Canada, and their sheer presence would deter the Americans from expanding northwards into empty country. Between 1885 and the outbreak of the First World War in 1914, hundreds of thousands of European immigrants crossed the Atlantic for a new life in Western Canada.

Agricultural immigration was encouraged most vigorously under the direction of Clifford Sifton (Minister of the Interior in Wilfrid Laurier's government from 1896 to 1905), and during the first decade of the 1900s the stream of immigrants

became a flood. Experienced farmers were attracted from the American Plains, where good land was becoming scarce and expensive, but they were too few to fill the vacant lands that stretched west from Winnipeg. In Britain, recruitment efforts were focused on attracting immigrant farmers from the harsh northern regions of Scotland and Yorkshire, rather than

POSTER DISTRIBUTED BY THE CANADIAN GOVERNMENT AND THE CPR TO ATTRACT IMMIGRANTS TO WESTERN CANADA.

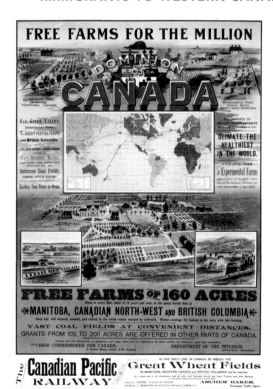

from the larger populations of southern cities. When journalists and politicians complained that foreign immigrants were taking up land that could be made available to the unemployed of Eastern Canada, Sifton replied: "Experience shows that workingmen from the cities and towns are the most helpless people in the world when they are placed upon the Prairie and left to shift for themselves." His view of a desirable immigrant was "a stalwart peasant in a sheep-skin coat born on the soil, whose forefathers have been farmers for ten generations, with a stout wife and a half-dozen children."

With this view in mind, promotional pamphlets and flyers extolling the wonders of Western Canada were printed in several European languages. In Central and Eastern Europe, governments that were concerned about losing their farmers would not allow Canadian immigration officials to talk to their citizens; instead, the immigration officers gave bonuses to the agents of railway and steamship lines to entice local people to come to Canada. Such efforts were particularly fruitful in the Austro-Hungarian provinces of Galicia and Bukovina, an area roughly equivalent to today's western Ukraine. The "Galicians," as Ukrainian immigrants were usually known in Canada, fit the image of the stalwart peasants that Canadian advertisements sought to attract for Prairie settlement, and many were receptive to Canadian propaganda. With a growing population in the Ukraine, rural people were forced to choose between trying to support more workers from the same small farms or migrating to join the unemployed in the cities of Eastern Europe. The fact that the Galicians were taxed and governed by foreign and German-speaking rulers further motivated them to

consider venturing to a distant country that promised free land and democratic government.

Galician immigrants were subject to much the same hardship, confusion and cultural shock that had faced settlers from the British Isles and Western Europe who had cleared the farm lands of Eastern Canada during the nineteenth century. By the early twentieth century, crossing the ocean by steamship was much quicker and more comfortable, and the Canadian government had assembled an infrastructure of railway transportation and immigration halls that had not been in place for earlier settlers. On the other hand, the Galicians came from a culture and society that were radically different from those of early twentieth-century Canada, and they suffered to a greater degree the dislike and prejudice of those who had arrived from other countries and in earlier decades.

Galician immigrants, their children and grandchildren distinguished themselves by writing extensively about their experiences, recording not only the events of their day-to-day lives but also the motives and thoughts that prompted people to tear themselves away from familiar surroundings and set out on a great endeavour. From what their stories tell us of the immigrant experience shared by all newcomers to Canada, we are able to imagine the travels and hardships of a typical Galician family whose destination was the newly opened farmland northeast of Edmonton.

Most Galicians emigrated from small rural villages where their families had lived for uncounted generations. By 1900, many such villages had pooled their money to send a family member to report on conditions in Canada, or an entire family may already have left to try its fortune in the new land. Emigrants often travelled in small groups of related families, with the assumption that others would follow if their letters gave favourable reports of the country. For some, the undertaking could be seen as going to a new Ukraine, one that they would build themselves in the company of relatives and friends. But with their hopes came fears and worries about the journey—and about the unknown land to which it was taking them. Was it really the promised country of rich farmlands given freely to all comers? What about the rumours of everlasting snow, of wolves and bears, Indian attacks and American train robbers? What if the border officials would not recognize their passports or refused to allow them to travel? What if the railway rejected their tickets? Most of the money that had been raised from the sale of property and livestock had gone to a railway agent in exchange for tickets for the train from Galicia across Poland and Germany, the steamship between Hamburg and Halifax, and another train from there to unknown places called Winnipeg, Saskatoon or Edmonton.

A FARMER BREAKING PRAIRIE SOD WITH A PLOUGH AND TEAM OF OXEN ABOUT 1900.

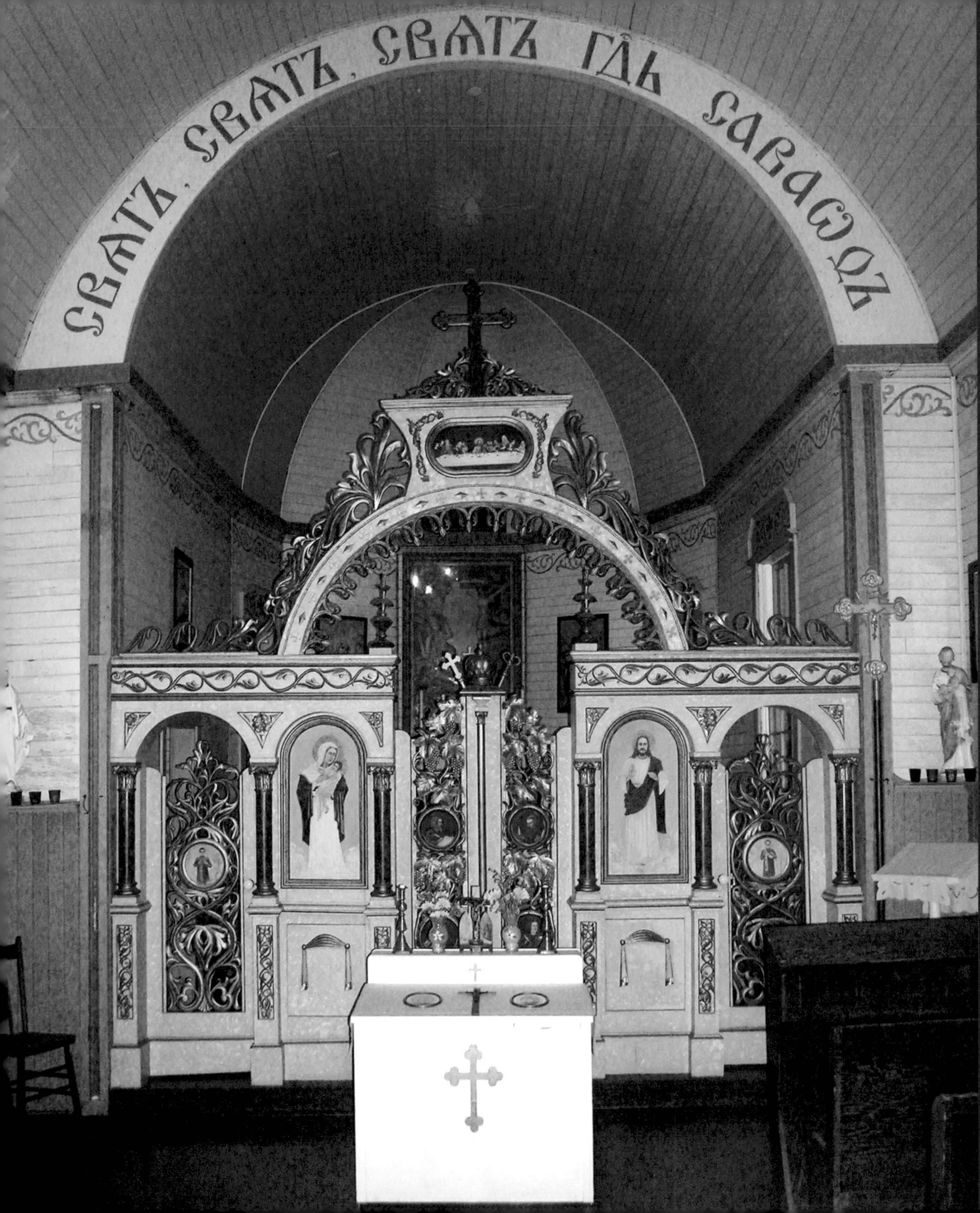
СВѦТЪ, СВѦТЪ, СВѦТЪ ГДЬ САВАѠѲЪ

THE INTERIOR OF ST. ONUPHRIUS CHURCH, WHICH WAS BUILT IN THE UKRAINIAN STYLE NEAR SMOKY LAKE, ALBERTA IN 1907. THE CHURCH WAS MOVED AND RECONSTRUCTED INSIDE THE CANADA HALL AT THE CANADIAN MUSEUM OF CIVILIZATION.

For those who had never before left a Ukrainian village, the journey across Europe would have been adventure enough. Even those who had travelled, and could speak some German, were bewildered by the immensity of Hamburg, the mass of docks and cranes and warehouses that they passed on their way to the port. Who could have known that there were so many iron ships, that they were so huge and that, despite their size, the sea could toss them so that green water foamed along the decks and down the hatches into the immigrant quarters? Most suffered a week of seasickness, followed by a few days of boredom and attempts to eat strange foods. Many shared the sadness when a child died of fever, and the subsequent outraged grief when the crew insisted that he or she be buried at sea. The immigration hall at Halifax was a confusion of voices speaking numerous languages, none of them understood by the officials. The families were herded through passport checks, a quick examination by a doctor who stamped their papers, and then on to the railway station and into a huge railway car with wooden benches and no private compartments.

The first days on this part of the journey were encouraging, travelling through the orderly farms and orchards of the Maritimes and the province of Quebec, seeing white-painted houses and well-fed horses in the fields and on the roads. Then, just when they had begun to believe that all the stories they had heard about Canada were true, the train turned north and for three days crawled through northern Ontario: a chaos of rocks and endless burned forests, the gullies filled with snowdrifts not yet melted in early summer. For most this was the low point of the journey, when they feared what they had long suspected: all the good land had been taken, and only wilderness remained for them. No one could answer their questions, their German was no longer of any use, and they were lost on a distant continent that was more barren than they had thought possible.

The despair lifted when they finally arrived in Manitoba and again saw thriving farmlands: flat open landscapes with tall grass and deep black soil. Everything looked new, but there were stone buildings and lines of telegraph poles stretching to the horizon, as well as tall grain elevators. Over the following days the train continued westwards through grasslands, the farms and trees becoming fewer and the ponds' white edging heralding a country too dry for farming. At Calgary, they were herded from the first train and led to another that travelled north, with a distant view in the west of mountains very like the High Carpathians. The track ended in Strathcona, across the river from the small town of Edmonton, and the families found their way to the immigration hall to spend the night. The men wandered the streets trying to find news of earlier emigrants, some of whom had begun arriving in wagons to meet their relatives from the train. There was a universal surge of relief to find someone from home, someone who could answer their worried questions, and who would help them on the last stage of their voyage.

The final part of their journey to the homestead took three or four days of walking and riding in the horse-drawn wagons provided by earlier settlers. The country just east of Edmonton was mostly cleared, and boasted fine wooden houses and barns. The families were rowed across the

Saskatchewan River in dangerous flat scows, then climbed the high banks to the north and continued along tracks cut through the bush. Here, the clearings were smaller and more recently made, the houses more makeshift and, when they finally arrived at their relatives' home, they were likely to find a simple hut of the kind used by the poorest itinerant labourer at home: a small dugout with a steeply pitched roof covered with grass and sod. Most families selected their quarter section (about 65 hectares) of land close to that already settled by relatives or friends, and had their help in building a dugout shelter and planting a garden in a patch of bush that had been cleared by fire a few years before.

The hut became the centre of their lives for the first two or three years, a time of unending work and much misery. The long summer days were spent chopping trees, clearing stumps and stones, scything hay from the beaver meadows to sell or to exchange for a borrowed horse and plough, building fences to keep rabbits and deer from the rows of cabbages, onions, carrots and garlic grown from seeds brought from home. People who had spent their lives in well-ordered villages were unfamiliar with loneliness and mosquitoes, with working every day of the week, and eating outside in the evening dusk to the sounds of unfamiliar frogs and owls. The first harvests of hand-sown rye and barley were soon cut by scythe, and the men took jobs stooking sheaves for established farmers to the south of the river, who cut their wheat with horse-drawn binders and separated the grain with steam-driven threshing machines. Autumn drove away the mosquitoes, and was a glorious season to work in the golden-leafed forests— save for the worry that the coming winter would outlast the

family's meagre stores of food. Most of the men left to look for winter jobs in the new coal mines west of Edmonton, or building roadbeds for the approaching railway, working with shovel and wheelbarrow for a dollar a day. For the women, winter was a ceaseless round of chopping wood to feed the clay stove that filled the back corner of the hut, breaking ice to get water from the creek, baking bread with poorly milled grain, and constantly watching young children. Often, boys and girls had no boots and so they stayed indoors for weeks at a time, playing and squabbling on the clay floor or on the large clay stove where they slept for warmth.

The memories of those first years gradually faded once the family moved into a new log house, plastered and trimmed with sawn and painted lumber. Life improved greatly with a good roof, an iron cookstove, a well dug in the yard, and a log barn for the cows, chickens and team of horses. Men began talking of buying binders, leasing a threshing machine, and getting larger wagons to haul their grain to the railway. Within a very few years, the families in the district built a school and hired a Ukrainian teacher, trained in Manitoba, to hold classes during the months between seeding and harvest, when the days were warm and long enough for the young-sters to walk there and back and still have time for chores. The school brought in a few of the children of English and Scandinavian settlers nearby, and the Ukrainian kids quickly learned English. Now that they had the church, and all of the neighbours gathered for Christmas Eve, the wild cold land was beginning to feel like home.

June 21, 1919

12. *Winnipeg 1919*

June 21, 1919

The midsummer sun rose to reveal a brilliant Saturday morning, but the city was unusually quiet. No streetcars rumbled along the streets carrying sleepy workers to factories and shops, no horse-drawn wagons delivered milk or bread, and no police patrolled the sidewalks. The city had been on strike for almost six weeks, and the significance of that fact had finally been noticed by the federal government in Ottawa. The events that would occur later in the day focused the attention of the country, and much of the world, on this booming Prairie city. If a single day can be said to mark a change in the fortunes of a city, this was the day that Winnipeg would remember.

IMMIGRANTS ARRIVING IN WINNIPEG BY TRAIN.

Canada is today one of the most urbanized nations on Earth. Each of its cities takes pride in its unique culture and way of life, a style that developed in large part from the city's origin, its reasons for existing, and the pace of its development. Montréal began as a tiny fur-trading post in the 1640s, and grew slowly for more than 150 years before it could truly be called a city. Toronto was founded in 1793 on the whim of a governor who judged it suitable for the administrative capital of a new colony; decades later it was still a small town with notoriously muddy streets. The pace of urban development increased during the nineteenth century, with the onset of massive immigration and advances in industry and transportation technologies. The cities of Eastern Canada were the first to experience the waves of immigration, the rapid growth of factories powered by steam and water, the sudden prominence of bankers, financiers and real-estate dealers. But the most astonishing example of urban development occurred far to the west, where Winnipeg grew from the tiny villages of the Red River Valley to become Canada's third-largest city within the span of a single generation.

When the province of Manitoba joined the Canadian Confederation in 1870, as a result of the Red River Rebellion, the Hudson's Bay Company's fort at the junction of the Red and Assiniboine Rivers was selected as the seat of government. The fort was the focus of a small community of about 100 people occupying a score of ramshackle houses, hotels and stores serving the farming and Métis communities of the Red River Valley. The new province attracted an influx of English-speaking immigrants to the area, some from Britain but most from the established farmlands of Ontario,

and these newcomers soon replaced the French-speaking Métis and the descendants of early Scottish colonists as the dominant force in determining the future of the community. In 1873, the rapidly growing Anglo-Protestant population incorporated the City of Winnipeg when it was a town of no more than 3,000 people, most of them single men. The new city had suddenly sprung up from the flat landscape on the west bank of the Red River, a small cluster of wood-frame buildings lining a few wide black-mud streets.

This jerry-built, flood-prone and mosquito-plagued "city" had no better prospects for future growth than had several other small towns in the Red River Valley. Winnipeg's links to the outside world were limited to canoe or York boat, Red River cart, and three small steamboats operating on the Red River. The key to expansion would be the eventual route chosen for the Canadian Pacific Railway (CPR), and towns such as Selkirk, downstream from Winnipeg, appeared to have better chances in the early running. However, in 1879, a railway line was completed from Winnipeg to Emerson on the American border, where it was linked to the expanding American railway system. Two years later, after an intense lobbying campaign by local enthusiasts, the CPR decided that its transcontinental track would cross the Red River at Winnipeg. The next two years saw a boom in land sales and property values that at one point outpaced those of Chicago. Writer and economist Stephen Leacock, whose father travelled from Ontario to take part in the excitement, wrote: "If ever there was a fool's paradise, it sure was located in Winnipeg. Men made fortunes—mostly on paper—and life was one continuous joy ride."

LOOKING NORTH ALONG WINNIPEG'S MAIN STREET IN 1874. DURING THE FOLLOWING DECADE, THE VILLAGE WAS TRANSFORMED INTO A CITY THAT WAS THE TRANSPORTATION HUB OF WESTERN CANADA.

Not all of the fortunes to be made were illusory, and by the time land values plummeted in 1882, several local men had accumulated large sums of capital. Much of this was invested in the development of local enterprises, in the construction of houses, civic and commercial buildings, streetcar lines, electric utilities, and other requirements of a modern city. By 1885, the population had grown to 20,000, civic leadership and the local press were firmly in the hands of Ontario-born Protestants, and Winnipeg was a bulwark of opposition to the Métis rebellion that flared that summer along the Saskatchewan River Valley. The defeat of the Métis, and the disappearance of the buffalo, which had forced the Plains Indians onto reserves, heralded the triumph of farming and agricultural immigration as the future of Western Canada. Winnipeg was at the centre of the new railway lines bringing immigrants and manufactured goods from the east, and exporting the wheat that was rapidly becoming the foundation of the Prairie economy.

The great swell of western immigration occurred between 1898 and 1913, coinciding with a string of successful wheat harvests and abundant capital investment from Britain and Eastern Canada. New railway lines fanned out across the wheat lands, and were soon dotted with small towns and grain elevators. Everyone and everything passed through Winnipeg on its way to and from Eastern Canada and the markets of Europe. Railway shops and shipping terminals expanded across the northern edge of the original townsite. The area south of the tracks now became the heart of the wholesale and retail businesses that supplied the machinery, construction materials, household goods and everything else required by thousands of Prairie farmers and hundreds of small railway towns. At the centre of the city stood the Grain Exchange, one of the world's most exciting financial markets, surrounded by imposing buildings housing the banks, insurance companies and other institutions that handled the finances of Western Canada.

Winnipeg had also become the labour exchange for the entire northwest, supplied by those arriving on the immigration trains and the crowds of transient workers looking for seasonal employment on farms or in the bush, in railway construction or in the growing industries of the city itself. Hotels, saloons and brothels spread throughout the areas where men congregated for employment. Flour mills, meat-packing plants, and factories processing food products or building machinery for the railway and the farm were clustered on the other side of the Red River in the old town of St. Boniface. The railway town of 40,000 people in 1900 had, by 1913, grown to over 150,000.

Throughout Winnipeg's early decades, the city's incessant growth had sustained an atmosphere of confident optimism that permeated the speeches of local politicians, newspaper editorials, and the promotional literature of business associations. Writers and speakers constantly quoted figures reporting Winnipeg's growth rate, miles of streetcar track constructed, tonnes of grain transported, and the city's rising net worth. Winnipeg was constantly compared to Chicago, and it seemed unthinkable that its future would be any less bright than that of the hub of the American Midwest. In fact, many of the city's opinion leaders assumed that Winnipeg had one great advantage over Chicago: it was a northern Anglo-Saxon city with a hardworking and reliable Protestant population who were determined to build a society on the solid British values that had made England the envy of the world. The discrepancy between this assumption and the reality of Winnipeg in the early twentieth century would gradually become apparent.

By the early 1900s, Winnipeg had become two cities divided by the CPR's extensive rail yards. To the south of the tracks lay the commercial and financial heart of the city and the residential quarters of the middle classes; prosperous Anglo-Manitobans had now retreated further south to the leafy regions beyond the Assiniboine. North of the tracks was the North End, a region of overcrowded shacks and slum housing inhabited mainly by immigrants. Most were either unemployed or worked in the low-wage industries that were making Winnipeg a manufacturing as well as a transportation centre. Poverty and its related diseases (worsened by a lack of piped water and sewage systems) were endemic. Reports of life in the North End read much like a multilingual version of Charles Dickens's descriptions of the London slums, written half a century earlier, with the ever-present gin replaced by cheap whisky. Through long agreement with the police force,

NORTH WEST MOUNTED POLICE PREPARE TO CONFRONT THE STRIKERS AT PORTAGE AND MAIN STREETS ON BLOODY SATURDAY, 1919.

sections of the North End were also allotted to the many brothels and saloons serving the huge migrant labour population that surged through the city: as many as 25,000 men arrived each summer on special trains from Eastern Canada to harvest and thresh the Prairies' wheat crop.

The CPR rail yards could not separate the two cities of Winnipeg forever, no matter how convenient such a partition was for those living to the south of the tracks. Organizations such as the All Peoples' Mission, directed by J.S. Woodsworth (who would go on to lead Canada's first federal socialist party), insisted that Winnipeggers living south of the railway tracks learn about the appalling conditions under which people lived in the North End. Winnipeg participated in the moral crusade that swept North America during the first decade of the twentieth century, which was led by the temperance movement's campaign to ban the sale of alcohol. The reformers portrayed the North End as a city of iniquity that had to be reformed, regardless of its residents' wishes. The clash of cultures became increasingly bitter throughout the decade beginning in 1910.

Economic depression began to afflict Canada in 1913, and the low-wage workers of Winnipeg were hit by rising unemployment. The following year brought the onset of the First World War, with rising prices for food and other necessities but no increase in wages. Large numbers of young men from all areas of Winnipeg enlisted in the Canadian Armed Forces, but enthusiasm for the British cause and support for conscription was far higher among Anglo-Manitobans than among the poverty-stricken multi-ethnic immigrant community of the North End. Mistrust of the newcomers and disbelief in their commitment to the war was manifest in the *War Measures Act* of 1914, which defined Ukrainians, and other immigrants from Eastern Europe who had originally lived under the rule of the far-flung Austro-Hungarian Empire, as enemy aliens. Over 80,000 people in Canada, many of them from Winnipeg, were registered with the police and required to live with parole-like restrictions on their movements and employment. Over 8,000, most of them unemployed young men, were interned in prison camps in the forests of British Columbia, northern Ontario and Quebec, where they provided labour for railway construction, mining and forest clearing.

The conclusion of the war in 1918 brought little relief to the North End. There were signs that Winnipeg would not regain the prosperity that it had experienced before the war, partly because the 1915 opening of the Panama Canal had transformed the transportation systems of western North America. Shipping grain through the port of Vancouver was now more efficient than freighting it eastwards to Great Lakes boats and then transshipping it to ocean-going vessels bound for European markets. Winnipeg's industry and commerce were so closely tied to its position as a transportation centre that most local factories and business enterprises suffered from the decline in rail traffic. Returning soldiers, as well as the men released from internment camps, increased the numbers of unemployed workers and enabled managers to maintain wages at low levels. The influenza pandemic of 1918–1919 was particularly destructive in Winnipeg's North End, where people contracting the disease died at about twice the rate of those in the southern regions of the city.

In the spring of 1919, as the influenza pandemic ran its course, Winnipeg's two cities were finally forced to confront one another. The unemployed and low-wage workers of the North End now included large numbers of men who had spent the past five years in the army or in prison camps. They had seen parts of the world far from Winnipeg, had met and worked alongside men from vastly different backgrounds, and had listened to people who had new ideas about how workers should be treated. Russia had been transformed into the Soviet Union barely a year before. The new socialist state's ideals were seen by working people as a beacon of hope for a new age, while the cruelty and destruction of the revolution that had brought it to power appalled Canada's governing classes. Throughout North America, workers who had recently returned from the trenches of Europe were involved in increasingly aggressive conflicts with the owners of mines and factories.

By the end of the war, most of Winnipeg's skilled workers were represented by a variety of trade unions, but a new force now appeared with the One Big Union movement, which aspired to represent the interests of both unskilled labourers and skilled workers in all industries. The movement had communist associations but, more importantly, it was seen by Winnipeg's workers as a uniquely Western endeavour that would support them against both the employers and the trade unions based in Eastern Canada. The owners and managers of Winnipeg's factories, on the other hand, saw the One Big Union as a communist front, aimed at nothing less than an overthrow of the entire capitalist system and the imposition of a worker-led state.

The final clash of communities began on May 1, 1919, when metal and construction workers struck for better wages and improved working conditions. In the enthusiasm following May Day celebrations, and in keeping with the ideals of One Big Union, the trade-union leaders called for a sympathetic strike by other workers to begin on May 15. Over 25,000 left their jobs, bringing the majority of businesses and transportation systems to a standstill. They were joined or supported by most city workers, including the police, firemen and waterworks employees. Civic leaders saw the strike not as an attempt to improve working conditions, but as a revolutionary coup led by communist immigrants who meant to take over the city—if not the country. These fears were heightened when the Strike Committee arranged for the police to continue patrolling, and for other strikers to carry out vital services such as firefighting and milk delivery. Four days later, the employers and civic officials of southern Winnipeg founded a volunteer Citizen's Committee of One

FIRE HOSES ARE BROUGHT INTO PLAY BY CITIZENS WHO OPPOSED THE STRIKE

Thousand to police the strikers, whom they characterized as alien Bolsheviks. The following six weeks saw numerous skirmishes between vigilantes and strikers, both groups led by veterans of the recent war. Telegrams and politicians flowed back and forth between Winnipeg and Ottawa and, as the standoff continued, the federal government became increasingly convinced that they were facing the beginnings of a socialist revolution. New legislation on sedition and the deportation of immigrants was rushed through Parliament. Winnipeg's North West Mounted Police detachment was quickly strengthened, as was the Canadian military presence in the city.

On June 17, ten strike leaders were quietly arrested under the new laws and removed to prison. The following Saturday, the mounted police were summoned to control a meeting called by war veterans who were in sympathy with the strike. A large crowd gathered in front of Winnipeg's city hall, the *Riot Act* was read by the mayor, and the mounted police charged the stone-throwing crowd three times—the third time with handguns drawn and firing. Two strikers were killed and many wounded, a streetcar was set ablaze, and the streets were cleared by hundreds of club-wielding "special police" supplied by the Citizen's Committee. By the time the army arrived with machine guns, the crowd had dispersed, but the show of overwhelming force, and the federal government's resolve to use it, had had its effect. The strike was called off a few days later, leaving a resounding bitterness that echoed down the years of economic depression and civic decline that followed. However, the events of Bloody Saturday, and the strike that produced them, left a more important legacy to the country as a whole. Among those who led the campaign for social reform in the following decades, and who eventually brought about a transformation in the Canadian sense of social justice, were many who were driven by the outrage and unfairness that they had originally felt as leaders and sympathizers of the Winnipeg General Strike.

By July 1, 1919—Dominion Day—Winnipeg had survived the war, the influenza pandemic, and the most extensive and significant labour action in Canada's history. The city's days of seemingly boundless growth and prosperity were over, but it had been quite the ride. Local people who could recall memories of buffalo herds roaming across endless wild prairie were now only middle-aged. Their childhood village of Métis hunters and Scottish fur traders had been transformed first into a western version of an Ontario town, then suddenly into the most booming and ethnically diverse metropolis in the country. Winnipeg's future development would never again be as explosive, but it would never again be as divided as it was in June 1919.

13. *Wheat, Dust, and Politics*

August 23, 1935

The headline in the Boston Globe *read "Alberta Goes Crazy!" The editors of the* Calgary Herald *and* Edmonton Journal *were shocked and disappointed. As the votes from the previous day's election were tallied, it had become apparent that the newly formed Social Credit Party had won an overwhelming victory, taking all but 7 of the 63 seats in the provincial legislature. Throughout the province, people awakened to hope that the Depression could now be beaten, or to fear that Alberta had taken a path towards economic chaos.*

THE WINNIPEG GRAIN EXCHANGE: AN INSTITUTION THAT
WAS VIEWED WITH DEEP SUSPICION BY WESTERN FARMERS.

The new Social Credit Party gave voters more than the usual vague assurances about honesty, good government and wealth. The Social Credit movement took its name from the economic theories of an eccentric English engineer who had developed a new, and previously untried, means of achieving the prosperity that all politicians promised to deliver. This was based on the belief that there was an imbalance between the volume of goods that could be produced by a modern industrial economy and the amount of money available to buy such goods, and that this discrepancy could be corrected by injecting more money into the economic cycle. A majority of Albertans who voted for Social Credit believed that the new government would provide them with a benefit of $25 per month, an amount that would approximately double the income of a farm family.

Social Credit's success in the 1935 election was largely due to the character and methods of its leader, William "Bible Bill" Aberhart, a schoolteacher turned evangelical preacher who pioneered religious radio broadcasting in Alberta. Learning of Social Credit in 1932, Aberhart gradually turned his Sunday broadcasts into a pulpit from which he could both save the souls of his listeners and rescue them from an economic system that had given them only "poverty in the midst of plenty." This blend of religion and financial theory proved compelling for Albertans whose lives had been disrupted by five years of drought, grasshoppers, and an economy that seemed to produce mainly unemployment or, for those lucky enough to keep their jobs, lower wages. Aberhart's spellbinding rhetoric crystallized the sense shared by most Prairie people that something had unaccountably gone wrong; the

promise of a new land where hard work and ingenuity would be rewarded by a secure—and perhaps prosperous—life had turned to ashes.

All of Canada had been battered by the Depression of the 1930s, but none had felt its blows more severely than the Prairie farmers who faced assault from both the climate and the international economic situation. Wheat had opened up the Canadian Prairies to settlement in the decades around the beginning of the twentieth century. By 1904, the Prairies were producing two million tonnes of wheat; this amount had almost doubled by 1906 and doubled again by 1913. In 1907, the Canadian government's experimental farms developed Marquis wheat, a strain that could be grown as far north as the Peace River country of northeastern British Columbia, had excellent baking qualities, and became the heart of the Canadian wheat industry during the early twentieth century. Despite occasional years of drought or wheat blight, and others in which markets were glutted and the price paid for wheat barely covered farmers' costs, the grain industry developed rapidly. By the 1920s, the Canadian Prairies were providing over 40 per cent of the wheat sold on international markets.

Prairie farmers saw themselves as independent producers, as the foundation of the market economy that supported the entire nation. These families were willing to take their chances on drought, hail and blight, and to persevere through hard work in the hope of a better future. Yet grain farmers knew that their work was enmeshed in a complicated economic system over which they had as little control as they had over the weather. The politics of 1935 were rooted in half a century of growing conflict between Prairie farmers, the grain industry that purchased their produce, the railways that transported it, and the financial institutions that funded the entire operation. The price at which the large grain companies bought wheat from farmers was set at a seemingly arbitrary rate through the mysterious workings of the Winnipeg Grain Exchange, an organization that farmers saw as a combination of a cartel and gambling casino. The costs charged by the railways for transporting grain to shipping ports were set by railway managers based in Eastern Canada. Interest rates on farm mortgages and loans for farm machinery were established at banking headquarters in Montréal and Toronto. The federal government in Ottawa maintained a system of tariffs that forced farmers to purchase machinery manufactured by Ontario companies, rather than importing cheaper models from the United States. The individual Western farmer had no say in any of these matters.

It was this situation that had prompted farmers to organize co-operative enterprises that lowered costs through wholesale purchasing of seed grain, binder twine, farm machinery and other necessary goods. The co-operative movement found fertile soil in the Prairies, and local groups quickly merged into provincial-level organizations that could challenge the power of the grain buyers and the railways. By 1906, Saskatchewan and Manitoba farmers had formed the Grain Growers' Grain Company, which purchased a seat on the Winnipeg Grain Exchange and began to grade and market the grain produced by its members. The United Farmers of Alberta (UFA) was organized in 1909 as a federation that not

only represented the economic interests of Alberta farmers but also strove to build a harmonious society.

To the UFA, the farmer was "both capitalist and labourer," and was therefore in a unique position to lead society to the realization that progress lay not through class conflict but through the co-operative efforts of all classes. Farmers' federations across the Prairies combined the principles of the co-operative movement with elements of the "social gospel," a form of Christian practice that emphasized the importance of social justice and the improvement of living and working conditions for all members of society. From this, it was a short step to political involvement and, in 1919, the UFA converted itself into a political party. In the 1921 provincial election, the UFA elected a sizeable majority, and would form the government of Alberta for the next 14 years. Similar farm-based parties elected members to the provincial governments in Saskatchewan and Manitoba, and sent reform-minded representatives to the federal Parliament.

The 1920s was a period of optimism for Western farmers, despite periodic droughts and depressions in the price of wheat. Wheat pools were organized in all three provinces, in order to obtain a better and more stable price by co-operatively marketing the grain produced by a large number of farmers. Agriculture began to be mechanized, and the rapid spread of gasoline-powered tractors and combine harvesters allowed farmers to cultivate much larger acreages. In 1928, the farm income in Alberta was the highest in Canada, and the average farmer could count on a profit that was roughly the same as the salary of a senior high-school teacher. Yet by the late

The worldwide Depression of the 1930s began with the collapse of stock markets that occurred in the autumn of 1929. The brunt of the Depression began to be felt by Prairie farmers in 1930, when the prices paid for wheat dropped by over 50 per cent. The wheat pools went bankrupt and farmers keeping their grain in the hope of better prices found only further declines, with 1933 prices more than 70 per cent lower than those of 1929. At the same time, the climate turned on farmers throughout the region, with drought, hail, dust storms and grasshopper plagues destroying the crops year after year. Farmers who were paying off debts at the fixed-interest rates of the 1920s were soon destitute and, in the worst-hit regions, even those without debts could barely make ends meet. Large areas of southwestern Saskatchewan and southeastern Alberta were left almost deserted. Farm families abandoned their land in despair, moving to the northern fringes of the Prairies in search of better land or joining the unemployed seeking work or relief in the cities.

By the mid-1930s, it was clear that the established political parties controlling both provincial and federal governments could not solve the problems besetting Prairie farmers or, indeed, the entire country. It was time to search elsewhere for solutions and to look at political and economic systems outside the narrow range espoused by the ruling parties. The Social Credit idea of a government that handed out cash or credits to its citizens in order to bring the economy back into balance was not as bizarre as it may sound. Many economists and politicians of the period were calling for government action to increase the purchasing power of consumers. Some promoted schemes involving printing more money in order

1920s, many farmers across the Prairies had acquired considerable debts through purchasing more land and the machinery to cultivate it. Paying off these debts would have been a simple matter had conditions for farming and selling grain remained as they had been through the 1920s, but this was not to be.

THE SOCIAL GOSPEL OF THE CCF WAS SPREAD
ACROSS THE PRAIRIES AT MEETINGS SUCH AS THIS
PICNIC, WHERE TOMMY DOUGLAS WAS A SPEAKER.

to cause inflation, which would allow farmers to sell grain at higher prices while paying off their debts at the old fixed rates of interest. As it turned out, Alberta's Social Credit government made only a few attempts to introduce its "funny money" policies, and these were disallowed by the courts as infringing on federal monetary and banking legislation.

Other groups were beginning to explore social and economic solutions that went beyond simple tinkering with the money supply. In 1932 while William Aberhart was beginning to preach Social Credit from his pulpit at the Calgary Prophetic Bible Institute, the city hosted a meeting that attracted a broad range of Prairie farm and labour organizations with socialist interests. These groups united around the figure of J.S. Woodsworth, a Methodist minister who had long practised the social gospel in Winnipeg, had been jailed as a leader of the 1919 Winnipeg General Strike, and was now a federal member of Parliament. A decision was taken to form a social democratic political party that would work towards a "co-operative commonwealth," in which elected governments would play a greater role than individual capitalists in planning and managing the economy and welfare of the population. The following year, the Co-operative Commonwealth Federation (CCF) held their first convention in Regina, and drafted a manifesto that foresaw a nation in which "the principle regulating production, distribution and exchange will be the supplying of human needs and not the making of profits." By 1938, the CCF had formed the official opposition to the Saskatchewan government and, in 1944, swept the province on a policy advocating public health care.

The political parties formed across the Prairies during the 1930s, and the social and economic ideals to which they aspired, did not disappear with the end of the Depression. The CCF governed Saskatchewan for 20 consecutive years. In 1961 it converted itself into the New Democratic Party

(NDP), which continues to be a major political force in all Western provinces save Alberta. In federal politics, the NDP still advocates policies first stated in the Regina Manifesto of 1933, and has been instrumental in promoting much of Canada's social legislation related to health care and protection of the more vulnerable members of society. The Social Credit Party governed Alberta continuously from 1935 until 1971, for most of that time under the leadership of Aberhart's disciple and successor Ernest Manning. Over this period of 36 years, Social Credit was transformed from a fringe movement with unconventional economic philosophies into a stable party that firmly embraced capitalist ideals, efficient government, and a respect for the grassroots members from which its support came. Under Ernest Manning's son Preston, who founded and led the federal Reform Party during the 1990s, these ideas were brought to Ottawa and continue to influence federal politics.

Alberta and Saskatchewan were the regions of Canada most harshly affected by the Depression and by the rogue weather of the "dirty thirties." Each of these provinces chose its own path of social and economic survival, diverging in different directions from Canada's political mainstream. Both of these paths led to social and economic strategies that continue to have significant influence, not only on the farms and cities of the Prairies but also on Canada's development as a nation. We can now recognize that many of the social and economic policies that characterize the country today were forged in the drought and desperation of the Canadian Prairies during the 1930s.

July 1950

14. Yellowknife

July 1950

At midnight on a still summer evening, the Wildcat Cafe was closed, but life around it continued as usual. The glassy water of Great Slave Lake reflected the twilight sky, its mirror cracked by the rolling wake of a floatplane as it cut its engine and coasted towards the docks. The sudden silence was broken by the banter of men loading other planes with tents, groceries, drums of gas, a canoe, the engine of a portable drilling rig. Pilots spread maps on gas drums, discussing their destinations with prospectors and geologists heading off to camps scattered across the Barren Grounds.

THE SLOPE BEHIND THE FLOATPLANE DOCK WAS THE TRANSPORTATION AND OUTFITTING HUB OF OLD YELLOWKNIFE.

From up the granite hillside came the crash of empty bottles and the laughter of men who had just arrived after weeks in camp and were celebrating their freedom in the bar of the Old Stope Hotel. No one seemed to sleep on summer nights in Yellowknife. Constant daylight and good flying weather were too precious to waste.

In 1950, this restless town had only 15 years of history. Born out of a 1930s gold rush, it had grown as an unplanned scatter of cabins, shacks and makeshift shops sprawled around the original discovery site. By 1950, it had a modern hospital and school, and was developing a townsite that could have been found in suburban Edmonton. But Old Town, built on the bare granite hillsides around the floatplane docks and the Wildcat Cafe, remained much as it had been when gold was first found there. During the 1930s, the mines and logging camps of the northern bush had drawn workers from the jobless cities, Prairie farmers forced from their land by drought, men and women dreaming of striking it rich or simply escaping the Depression that afflicted the world economy. The resources of the North had transformed Canada's role from that of a simple supplier of wheat for Britain and Europe to that of a major exporter of gold, nickel, copper, lumber and newsprint feeding expanding world markets. The Second World War and the economic boom years that followed brought a greater need for these commodities, and towns like Yellowknife began to mushroom from Labrador to the Pacific Coast. Railroads snaked north towards the iron-bearing ranges of central Quebec and Labrador, the nickel deposits of northern Manitoba, and across Pine Pass to British Columbia's Peace River country

where the newly demilitarized Alaska Highway began its tortuous route through the Yukon.

Yellowknife was well placed to take advantage of this northern boom. Although it had no road or railway to the south, it was easily serviced by barge during the summer and by tractor train across the thick ice of Great Slave Lake in the winter. Even before its airstrip was built, huge Lancaster bombers that had survived the recent war in Europe roared down onto the ice and taxied to shore across from the Cafe, their bomb bays filled with groceries and construction materials. The advances that the war had brought to aircraft design and radio communications opened up immense areas of the North to prospectors and other travellers who flooded northwards in the early post-war years. The new Beaver and Otter bushplanes built by Canadian de Havilland could fly at any temperature, operate on either floats or skis, and land practically anywhere across the lake-strewn northland. The war had also produced many of the pilots who flew these aircraft, a group that had soon created a mythology based on skill, bravery and storytelling genius.

Although Yellowknife was built on gold, its development was fuelled by exploration of the mineral-rich lands stretching to the north and east as far as the Arctic Coast. In 1950, uranium was eagerly sought by governments needing fuel to develop the new enterprises of nuclear power and nuclear warfare. Canada's first major uranium strike had been on the shore of Great Bear Lake, 500 kilometres to the north of Yellowknife, and the best recent discoveries were around Lake Athabasca, a similar distance to the southeast. From the floatplane docks

at Yellowknife, prospectors fanned out northwards to explore the long-known copper deposits for which the Coppermine River had been named, and eastwards to investigate traces of gold, nickel and uranium recently discovered in the rocks of the Barren Grounds. There was talk of new oil fields down the Mackenzie River, of icebreakers opening the Northwest Passage to shipping, and of vast and mysterious military plans for the Far North. By 1950, Arctic Canada had become a strategic centre of the developing Cold War, as new long-range bombers carrying nuclear weapons became capable of reaching either the United States or the Soviet Union on trans-polar routes through Canadian airspace. Remote weather stations had been hastily established across the Arctic islands, and northern airfields were being extended to handle tankers refuelling the immense American bombers that cease-lessly patrolled the polar skies. Plans had also begun for a chain of radar stations along the Arctic Coast.

As the most northerly Canadian town with regular scheduled air service from the south, Yellowknife was the jumping-off point for many Arctic enterprises and the place that intro-duced many southerners to the Arctic. Here, workers from the south first experienced the extended daylight of the Arctic summer, the sun dipping behind the ridges north of town for only an hour at midnight. Here, they first encountered the Arctic winter's ice fog, brilliant auroras lighting the endless night, the howling of sled dogs, the makeshift buildings and raucous lifestyle of a latter-day Klondike. Yellowknife was a town of new arrivals. Most brought with them an image of the North formed from the poetry of Robert Service and the stories of Jack London, from Group of Seven

landscapes depicting rock and stunted trees, icebergs and barren mountains, and from romantic books and films starring Mounties and Eskimos, bush pilots and mad trappers. The reality of the North moulded itself to these images, developing the dimensions of a mythological land inhabited by legendary people.

This imaginary North of the 1950s was a magnet for artists and writers, as well as for miners and prospectors. In 1950 Farley Mowat had just returned south from his first journey to the Barren Grounds, and was writing the book that would bring him fame. *People of the Deer* told a marvellous tale of Dene caribou hunters, Métis trappers, and a small band of Inuit who lived and starved on the tundra to the west of Hudson Bay; it was read around the world, and for many Canadians created a yearning to experience the North. Across Hudson Bay, artist James Houston had just purchased a small collection of Inuit soapstone carvings and had introduced them to the art markets of North America, enthralling a public eager to believe that an ancient unspoiled world still existed in some distant region of the continent. Newspapers and magazines began to send journalists north. Among them was Pierre Berton, who was already working on the books that would appear later in the decade as *The Mysterious North* and *Klondike*, books that created a widespread fascination among Canadians for the history of the Far North.

Canada's vision of itself shifted northwards in the years around 1950. After the Second World War the view of Canada as a European colony, attempting to re-create Europe in the temperate regions of the New World, started to fade. Canadians began to develop a new perception of their country—that of a unique northern nation, whose destiny lay not in the cities and farmlands of the south, but in the forests, tundras and rocky plains stretching northwards to the frozen sea. By 1958, the government of John Diefenbaker had swept to power on the wings of a "Northern Vision." Diefenbaker, the orator from Prince Albert at the edge of the northern bush, compared himself to the country's first prime minister, John A. Macdonald, who opened up the West: "He saw Canada from east to west. I see a new Canada—a Canada of the North!" (February 12, 1958, Winnipeg).

Half a century later, northern Canada has become a far different place. Control over much of the land has now reverted to the Aboriginal occupants of the region, whose interests were largely ignored by the military and industrial planners of the 1950s, and whose plight first came to public attention through the writers and photographers of the time. Yellowknife, now the capital of the Northwest Territories, has become a government town with an imposing legislative building, high-rise office blocks, and a paved highway to the south. But these developments have had little impact on Old Town, the centre of activity in 1950. The Old Stope Hotel burned down long ago, and the beacon atop the granite hill above the floatplane docks has now been replaced by a monument to the many pilots who used that beacon to find their way home. But the Wildcat Cafe is once again open for business, and on summer nights the local docks are as busy as they were 50 years ago. A new generation of prospectors using a new generation of aircraft is now searching for diamonds, the latest bonanza of the Barren Grounds. Yellowknife is once again the exhilarating centre of northern hopes.

August 7, 1954

15. *New Faces*

August 7, 1954

The day was unusually hot and oppressive for Vancouver, but more than 25,000 people packed themselves into the newly completed Empire Stadium. The occasion was the British Empire and Commonwealth Games, and the world was tuned in to one event: the one-mile race between favourites Roger Bannister of England and John Landy of Australia. At small meets held earlier in the summer, each competitor had achieved a pace that athletes had long considered impossible: running the mile in less than four minutes. Now, for the first time and before a huge international audience, the two competitors were racing directly against each other in a field of top-ranked runners. Both finished the race in under four minutes: Bannister won in 3 minutes 58.8 seconds and Landy was less than a second behind.

A CREW OF CHINESE LABOURERS: ONE OF MANY WHICH WORKED ON THE WESTERN SECTIONS OF THE CANADIAN PACIFIC RAILWAY.

One hundred million people around the world listened to the race on radio, and for the first time in history a major sporting event was telecast internationally through a mix of microwave relays and film flown by aircraft to other continents.

These Games and their highlight, the "Miracle Mile," brought Vancouver to the attention of the world. The event also symbolized a turning point in both the Games and the city that hosted them. Before 1954, this event had been known as the British Empire Games and had attracted primarily white competitors from the British Isles, Canada, New Zealand, Australia, South Africa and Rhodesia (today's Zambia and Zimbabwe). The number of countries participating in the 1954 Vancouver Games had doubled, with teams from places as diverse as Jamaica, Uganda, Pakistan and Hong Kong. The change in name from "Empire" to "Empire and Commonwealth" had anticipated the growing independence of British colonies around the globe and the development of a more inclusive world order. Vancouver was witnessing this change in the competitions at Empire Stadium, on the streets of the city, and in the towns and work camps of the surrounding province.

British Columbia was proud of the heritage from which it took its name. Isolated by mountain ranges from the rest of Canada, it had developed a society and culture quite different from those to the east. Its British character stemmed from the influence of the Hudson's Bay Company (HBC), which was the major commercial force in the region during the first half of the nineteenth century. The HBC and its representatives were vigorous in combatting the political influence of the developing American states to the south, and co-operated with the English governors sent during the 1850s to administer the small colonies of Vancouver Island and British Columbia (formerly New Caledonia). The first assemblies appointed by these governors were largely composed of Company men, and colonial government was merely an extension of earlier rule by the HBC. The British naval base at Esquimalt and the regiment of Royal Engineers stationed at New Westminster reinforced the colonies' English character. Even after the colonies united and entered Canadian Confederation in 1871, they maintained a society that developed quite differently from that of Central and Eastern Canada.

This divergence was partially due to geography. With only small patches of land between the mountain ranges suitable for agriculture, British Columbia did not attract large numbers of British and European peasants seeking free land and a prosperous agricultural future, as happened in Eastern Canada and on the Prairies. The best farming land in British Columbia was owned by early immigrants, mostly from the British Isles or Northern Europe, and the resource industries that were to become the economic backbone of the province had their beginnings in enterprises developed by the same people. The vision of the country espoused by British Columbia's leaders was well expressed by R.E. Gosnell, a prominent provincial civil servant, who wrote that British Columbians were engaged in building "a greater Britain on the Pacific, where British arts and institutions will expand under fresh impetus, where the British flag will forever fly, where British laws and justice will be respected and enforced, and where British men and women will be bred equal to the best traditions of the race."

EMPIRE STADIUM AT THE TIME OF THE 1954 BRITISH EMPIRE AND COMMONWEALTH GAMES.

To achieve this goal, the farmers, ranchers, mine owners and early industrialists of British Columbia needed vast numbers of labourers, and preferably ones who were willing to work for low wages. In Eastern Canada during the nineteenth and early twentieth centuries, this sort of labour was provided by immigrants from Ireland and other European countries in which poverty was so widespread that even the difficult, dangerous, dirty and ill-paid jobs available in the eastern provinces were a better prospect than staying at home. Attracting European immigrants to British Columbia was more difficult, especially before the province was linked to the rest of Canada by the Canadian Pacific Railway (CPR) in 1885. However, vast

pools of willing labour were available across the Pacific, and poverty-stricken workers from East and South Asia soon began arriving to take the jobs that British Columbia offered.

The first arrivals were Chinese, mostly peasants from the overcrowded farmlands of southern Guangdong province, who joined the gold rush to the Fraser River during the late 1850s. Like most others who pursued the rumour of sandbars glistening with gold nuggets, almost all the Chinese venturers found little but hard labour and disappointment. Returning to China was not a possibility for men who could not afford a passage, and to many the hard conditions of the British Columbia frontier were preferable to those of a homeland devastated by the chaos and violence of the Opium Wars and the subsequent Taiping Rebellion. Many took jobs building wagon roads to the Cariboo goldfields, working for the few successful miners, providing labour for early sawmills and salmon canneries, or scraped a living in the small cities of Victoria and Vancouver.

The growing reputation of the Chinese as hard and honest workers attracted the builders of the CPR, and between 1880 and 1885 approximately 17,000 men were employed to construct the western sections of the track. Most arrived as members of labour gangs recruited by contractors from the peasant communities of southern China, and they usually sent their meagre wages home to support impoverished families. With the last spike driven and the CPR reneging on its contract to provide return passage, many of these men found themselves stranded in Canada. The few who could afford the fares brought their wives, children and other relatives to join them in their new home. Many scattered across the country, settling in cities and small towns as the operators of restaurants, laundries, general stores and other enterprises. Others dispersed to the mines, canneries, sawmills and farms of British Columbia, leading single lives devoted to hard work and saving the little they earned to send to their distant families.

Japanese peasant farmers and fishermen, as impoverished as those from China, missed the Fraser River gold rush, as their country was only beginning to emerge from the isolation created by an official policy of seclusion from the outside world. A few Japanese began arriving in British Columbia after 1885, mostly single men hoping to return home with a fortune quickly made in the forests and coal mines of Vancouver Island or the salmon fishery of the Fraser River. A decade later, a few young men began arriving from South Asia, mostly Sikhs from the villages of the Punjab who were particularly

drawn to work in the logging and lumber industry. Like their Chinese predecessors, these immigrants found that hard labour was poorly rewarded at the best of times, and that in periods of economic recession their presence in Canada was bitterly resented.

Apart from the early days of the Fraser River gold rush, the number of Asian immigrants in British Columbia never exceeded 10 per cent of the total provincial population. The hostility directed towards them by the white population was disproportionate to their numbers, and was more virulent than that experienced by Eastern European immigrants to the Prairies or Irish immigrants to Eastern Canada. As elsewhere, unskilled labourers perceived immigrants as unfair competition, willing to work for lower wages than those needed by local men to support their families. Most Anglo-Saxons of the time assumed that white Europeans were superior and the British Empire the pinnacle of human achievement. Non-white immigrants who came from impoverished peasant societies were easily dismissed as inferior peoples with corrupt cultures, who could never be assimilated into Canadian life. Moreover, white Canadians loudly voiced their fear that the Asians' ability to survive on low wages would eventually lead to lower local standards of living. Anti-Asian riots swept through Vancouver in 1887 and, more seriously, in 1907, when a parade by the Asiatic Exclusion League (a photograph of the parade shows a banner proclaiming "A White Canada and No Cheap Asiatic Labour") ended in beatings and the destruction of Asian-owned businesses.

THE *KOMAGATA MARU* WAS CHARTERED IN 1914 BY SIKH IMMIGRANTS, BUT THE SHIP WAS NOT ALLOWED TO DOCK IN CANADA.

Asians who succeeded in establishing themselves as successful farmers, fishermen and businessmen attracted the resentment of local competitors who were likely to have friends in municipal and provincial governments. The general view held by such people was articulated by a writer in a 1919 farming magazine, who stated that "the proportion of Orientals to whites in B.C. is too great, but only in one sense, and that is owing to the fact that they are in business for themselves and are not, as they should be, working for white men." From 1875 onwards, the British Columbia government passed numerous laws preventing Asian workers from being hired on public works projects, denying their right to vote in provincial elections, even prohibiting their admission to the provincial old-age home. British Columbia was not alone in these actions, as the governments of Saskatchewan and Ontario passed similar legislation.

The Government of Canada was not far behind. Prime Minister John A. Macdonald had realized that Chinese labour was necessary to open up Western Canada, and in 1882 defended the use of Chinese workers for construction of the CPR by telling Parliament that "either you must have this labour or you can't have the railway." However, when the CPR was completed in 1885, the federal government immediately instituted a "head tax" of $50 on any Chinese wishing to enter the country—a sum that was raised to $100 in 1900 and in 1903 to $500 (the equivalent of approximately $12,000 today). After the 1907 Vancouver riot, federal restrictions almost put an end to immigration from Asian countries. The

best-known example of this exclusionist policy was the 1914 incident of the *Komagata Maru*, a ship chartered by 376 Sikh immigrants to British Columbia, which was turned away without allowing its passengers to disembark. The federal government's strategy culminated in the *Chinese Immigration Act* of 1923, which virtually prevented further Chinese immigration and which required the registration of all Chinese already in the country. In 1920, Parliament legislated that Asians who were not British subjects could no longer vote in federal elections, although they were still liable for taxation and conscription on the same basis as other Canadians.

The belief in an "Oriental menace" to Canadian society held firm throughout the first half of the twentieth century, surfacing most damagingly after December 1941 when Japan attacked the American naval base at Pearl Harbor, captured Hong Kong and interned Canadian regiments defending the colony. Despite the absence of any evidence of Japanese-Canadian support for the new enemy, within months the federal government relocated over 20,000 people of Japanese descent from the coastal communities of British Columbia to internment camps in the interior and in Central Canada. With no dissenting voice from any Canadian political party, church or other organization, the government initiated the forced sale of farms, homes, businesses and over 1,100 fishing boats to non-Japanese owners. When the war ended in 1945, the government planned a mass deportation of Canada's Japanese population. That initiative was abandoned only after the matter was taken to the Supreme Court, but over 4,000 people had already left Canada for a new life amidst the ruins of a defeated Japan.

The situation changed rapidly in the years following the Second World War. China had been an ally of Canada during the war; large numbers of young Chinese Canadians had contributed to the Canadian military effort, and these returning veterans were not content to be denied the vote. Moreover, Canada's restrictions on its Asian citizens clearly contravened the Charter of the newly formed United Nations, which charged its members with "promoting and encouraging respect for human rights and for fundamental freedoms for all without distinction as to race, sex, language or religion." In 1947, the right to vote was extended to all citizens of Canada, whatever their ethnic origin (although the vote was not extended to Aboriginal Canadians, who were not considered to be citizens). In the same year, the *Chinese Immigration Act* was repealed, although it would be two decades before Asians were allowed to immigrate on the same basis as people from other parts of the world.

When the British Empire and Commonwealth Games focused the world's attention on Vancouver in 1954, British Columbia was experiencing the first hints of the changes that would transform its economy and society over the next half-century. Towns and cities across the province were increasing in size as another mining boom got underway, huge new smelting complexes were being planned, and forest industries were expanding to supply the growing market in North America and the reviving economy of Japan. Immigrants were again needed to dig coal, turn rock into ingots of metal, and transform trees into lumber or newsprint. The isolated bachelor work camps that had always been the skeleton supporting British Columbia's economy were now filled with

PART OF THE FLEET OF JAPANESE FISHING BOATS THAT WAS
EXPROPRIATED BY THE GOVERNMENT OF CANADA IN 1942.

The Thousand-Year Path 127

men escaping the post-war bleakness of Western Europe and the socialist states to the east. With the door at least partially open to immigrants from East and South Asia, many Asian Canadians who had endured the decades of isolation and hostility were now able to sponsor the arrival of their extended families. These in turn contributed to the success of businesses and industrial enterprises founded by earlier immigrants, and their children would develop into a new class of ethnically Asian entrepreneurs and professionals who would become active at all levels of Canadian society.

Other factors were at work in bringing rapid change to British Columbia. The development of long-range jet aircraft and the launch of mass air travel in the 1960s brought a new orientation to the world. Immigrants from Asia no longer travelled for days or weeks by ship, but reached Canada in a few hours and at a cost that was increasingly affordable. New Canadians from Pakistan to Korea could now maintain stronger links with their homelands, and people travelled regularly in both directions on business or for family visits. Business enterprises soon spanned oceans, as decisions and finances began to flow through rapidly developing telecommunication networks. Vancouver was no longer an isolated western outpost of Anglo-Saxon society; it had become the eastern terminus of a trans-Pacific economy and home to a multi-ethnic society thriving on its new economic strength.

Anyone who knew Vancouver half a century ago can still locate parts of the familiar city among the forest of glass towers, the cosmopolitan shops and restaurants, the demolition sites and urban wastelands. More difficult to find is any remnant of the British society of the 1950s and earlier decades, or of the attitudes that permeated and supported that society. It is a constant surprise to discover how quickly and how thoroughly human societies change, how the fears of one generation are transformed into the hopes and opportunities of the next. The value of history lies not in cataloguing the faults and horrors of the past, but in demonstrating the human capacity to transcend the past and create a society that is changed beyond recognition. If the worth of a culture is judged by its capacity to bestow dignity on all its citizens and to allow them to contribute to the best of their abilities, Vancouver's society today is without doubt superior to that of earlier generations.

Acknowledgements

As all who know me will readily admit, I am a historian in only the broadest sense of the term. I trained as an archaeologist, and most of my research and writing have related to the archaeology of the Indigenous peoples of Arctic North America. If this book has merit, it derives from the fact that an interested outsider has fewer limitations than does a dedicated historian. The interloper can scan the broad scope of a country's history, select topics and episodes that are of particular interest, and write about them in a manner that is not obscured by personal knowledge of the complexity of specific historical interpretations and reconstructions. For an awareness of these complexities, and to ensure the plausibility of my interpretations, I have relied heavily on my colleagues. Christina Bates, the late Jean-Pierre Chrestien, Ian Dyck, Jean-Pierre Hardy, Rhonda Hinther, Banseng Hoe, Chris Kitzan, David Morrison, Peter Rider and Patricia Sutherland have all read and provided valuable comments on one or more individual chapters. The entire manuscript was read by Victor Rabinovitch, whose editorial suggestions were constructive and much appreciated, as were those of editor Jennifer Rae-Brown. Carrie Dickenson is to be thanked for searching out and obtaining most of the images. I wish to express my gratitude to Sarah Lacharity, the late Deborah Brownrigg and Rosemary Nugent, who oversaw the project, and to Victor Rabinovitch, who first came up with the idea for such a book. If errors are found in the following text, despite all of the assistance that I have received, they can be ascribed solely to me.

Robert McGhee

Illustrations & Credits

Front cover –

Map: "Carte du Canada ou de la Nouvelle France…" par Guillaume Del'Isle
Source: Library and Archives Canada/NMC 11897
Canada Hall, IMG2008-0646-0001-Dm; IMG2008-0646-0002-Dm; IMG2008-0646-0003-Dm; IMG2008-0646-0004-Dm;IMG2008-0646-0005-Dm; IMG2008-0646-0006-Dm;IMG2008-0646-0007-Dm; IMG2008-0646-0008-Dm;IMG2008-0646-0009-Dm; IMG2008-0646-00010-Dm; IMG2008-0646-00011-Dm; IMG2008-0646-00012-Dm

Back cover -

Map: "Exhibiting all the New Discoveries in the Interior Parts of North America" by A. Arrowsmith, 1802
Source: Library and Archives Canada/NMC 019687-1

Preface left –

Map: "Carte du Canada ou de la Nouvelle France…" par Guillaume Del'Isle
Source: Library and Archives Canada/NMC 11897

Preface right –

Map: "Exhibiting all the New Discoveries in the Interior Parts of North America" by A. Arrowsmith, 1802
Source: Library and Archives Canada/NMC 019687-1

Ch. 1 & Acknowledgements –
The Royal Library Copenhagen—Ms. GKS 2881, 4°

Ch. 2 & 3 –
Carta del Cantino, Ms. membr., sec. 16. (ca. 1502), Biblioteca estense universitaria, Modena

Ch. 4 & TOC –
Map: "Carte de la Nouvelle France", Samuel de Champlain, 1632
Source: Library and Archives Canada/NMC 51970

Ch. 5 & 6 –
Map: "Carte du Canada ou de la Nouvelle France…" par Guillaume Del'Isle
Source: Library and Archives Canada/NMC 11897

Ch. 7-9 – Map: "Exhibiting all the New Discoveries in the Interior Parts of North America" by A. Arrowsmith, 1802
Source: Library and Archives Canada/NMC 019687-1

Ch. 10-12 – Map: "British America"
Source: Library and Archives Canada/NMC 017931

Ch. 13-15 – Reproduced with the permission of Natural Resources Canada 2008, courtesy of the Atlas of Canada.

p. 10 – Photo © Canadian Museum of Civilization/Robert McGhee, 1991—image IMG2008-0950-0003-Dm

p. 13 – Photo © Canadian Museum of Civilization/Robert McGhee, 2007—image IMG2008-0950-0005-Dm

p. 14 – Photo © Canadian Museum of Civilization/Robert McGhee, 2007—image IMG2008-0950-0004-Dm

p. 17 – The Royal Library Copenhagen—Ms. GKS 2881, 4°

p. 20 – Detail engraving: Whaling and Fishing Scene from Herman Moll's *Map of North America*, 1718—Library and Archives Canada/Maps Plans and Charts collection/CMC 3686

p. 21 – Bibliothèque National de France—Cartes et Plans, Rés. Ge AA 562

p. 23 – Carta del Cantino, Ms. membr., sec. 16. (ca. 1502), Biblioteca estense universitaria, Modena -Su concessione del Ministero per i Beni e le Attività Culturali-

p. 24 – Photo © Canadian Museum of Civilization/Robert McGhee, 1975—image IMG2008-0950-0002-Dm

p. 31 – "Whale Fishing": woodcut from Andre Thevet, *Cosmographie Universelle*, Paris 1574

p. 32 – Activity of a Basque whaling station in the Strait of Belle Isle around 1580, by Francis Back—S99-11,197

p. 36 – Voyages de Champlain Tome 3-4. Pg. 196 inset: Deffaite des Yroquois au lac Champlain, [1870]—Archives of Ontario, I0040051   971.011 CHB

p. 38 – Ville-Marie in 1685. Artist's conception by Francis Back for the book *Pour le Christ et le Roy, la vie au temps des premiers Montréalais*, 1992

p. 40 – Henri Chatelain, cartographer [ca.1719]. "Carte particulière du Fleuve Saint-Louis dressée sur les lieux avec les noms des sauvages du païs, des marchandises qu'on y porte & qu'on en reçoit…"—Archives of Ontario, I0004754 C 279-0-0-0-16

p. 44 – With permission of the Royal Ontario Museum © ROM 950.62.3: *Quebec from across the St. Lawrence* by Alicia Killaly—ROM2006_7705_1

p. 50 – "Dyke Land", imprint engraving by F.R. Schell—NSARM photo collection 200501862

p. 53 – Engraving from the Voyages of Samuel de Champlain, 1613: "Restoration of the Habitation of Port Royal, N.S." in the *Maritme Advocate and Busy East*, August 1940 — NSARM Scapbook Collection, MG 9, volume 36, p. 73 200501862

p. 56 – With permission of the Royal Ontario Museum © ROM 950.66.5: *View of Halifax taken in July 1757* by Benjamin Garrison—ROM2006_7707_1

p. 58 – With permission of the Royal Ontario Museum © ROM 955.218.4: *Market Wharf and Ferry Landing*, Halifax (watercolour) by William H. Eager—ROM2006_7754_1

p. 60 – Encampment of the Loyalists in Johnstown, a new settlement on the banks of the River St. Lawrence, in Canada West. J.R. Simpson [August 12, 1925]—Archives of Ontario, I0003081 RG 2-344-0-0-89

p. 66 – With permission of the Royal Ontario Museum © ROM 962.37: *Timber Raft on the St. Lawrence* (watercolour) by Frances Anne Hopkins—ROM2006_7822_1

p. 68 – Watercolour: Entrance of the Rideau Canal, Bytown, Upper Canada (Ottawa) February, 1839—Library and Archives Canada/ C-000518, Acc. No. 1955-128-11

p. 72 – Saskatchewan Archives Board—R-A3955

p. 74 – With permission of the Royal Ontario Museum © ROM 912.1.26: *Métis Running Buffalo* by Paul Kane—ROM2005_5147_1

p. 81 –   Josiah Bruce Metropolitan Methodist Church, Queen and Church Streets, Toronto [ca.1890]—Archives of Ontario, I0001872 F 1125-1-0-0-109

p. 82 –   Orange Parade, George Irwin—Archives of Ontario, I0014122 C 119-1-0-0-15

p. 82 –   An Orange parade on Queen Street West at Palmerston Avenue, Toronto [ca.1900] William H. Hammond fonds—Archives of Ontario, I0021921 F 4436-0-0-0-116)

p. 86 –   Photo: "Galician Settlers: Theodosy Wachna and family, Stuartburn, Manitoba" [ca.1890–1917]—Library and Archives Canada/ Department of the Interior fonds/C-006605

p. 87 –   Poster: "Free Farms for the Million" [ca. 1890]—Library and Archives Canada C-095320

p. 89 –   Watercolour: *Breaking Prairie in July, Northwest Territory, Canada* (Arthur Field's place, about 5 miles northeast of Broadview) by Edward Roper, (1833–1909) — Library and Archives Canada C-013884, Acc. No. 1989-446-25

p. 90 –   Photo © Canadian Museum of Civilization/Robert McGhee, 2008—image IMG2008-0950-0001-Dm

p. 94 –   L.B. Foote, 466 23 Feb. 1927—Manitoba Archives SIS N2066

p. 96 –   Manitoba Archives SIS N10213

p. 98 –   University of Manitoba Archives & Special Collections UM_pc018_A81-012_070_7188_013_0001

p. 101 –   University of Manitoba Archives & Special Collections UM_pc018_A81-012_070_7188_009_0001

p. 104 –   University of Manitoba Archives & Special Collections UM_pc018_A81-012_073_7297_001_0001

p. 107 –   Glenbow Archives, NA-2457-1

p. 108 –   Glenbow Archives, NA-2378-15c

p. 109 –   Glenbow Archives, NA-2629-10

p. 112 –   Credit: Edmonton Air Museum Committee Coll/ NWT Archives N-1979-003: 0127

p. 114 –   Credit: Busse/NWT Archives N-1979-052: 4573

p. 116 –   Credit: Edmonton Air Museum Committee Coll/ NWT Archives N-1979-003: 0456

p. 120 –   Vancouver Public Library, Special Colllections, VPL 1773

p. 122 –   BC Sports Hall of Fame and Museum (1304.44)

p. 124 –   Photo: Stuart Thomson, Vancouver Public Library VPL 6225

p. 127 –   Photo: Leonard Frank, Vancouver Public Library VPL 3190